MIXED MARTIAL ARTS UNLEASHED

Mastering the Most Effective Moves for Victory

MICKEY DIMIC
TWO-TIME WORLD CHAMPION

with *Christopher Miller*

McGraw Hill

New York Chicago San Francisco Lisbon London Madrid Mexico City
Milan New Delhi San Juan Seoul Singapore Sydney Toronto

The *McGraw·Hill* Companies

Library of Congress Cataloging-in-Publication Data

Dimic, Mickey.
    Mixed martial arts unleashed : mastering the most effective moves for victory /
Mickey Dimic with Christopher Miller.
        p.   cm.
    Includes index.
    ISBN-13: 978-0-07-159890-3 (alk. paper)
    ISBN-10: 0-07-159890-1 (alk. paper)
    1. Mixed martial arts.   I. Miller, Christopher, 1977–   .   II. Title.

GV1102.7.M59D56   2009
796.815—dc22   2008008755

1 2 3 4 5 6 7 8 9 10 11 12 13 14 15 16 17 18 19 20 21 DOC/DOC 0 9 8

ISBN 978-0-07-159890-3
MHID   0-07-159890-1

McGraw-Hill books are available at special quantity discounts to use as premiums and
sales promotions or for use in corporate training programs. To contact a representative,
please visit the Contact Us pages at www.mhprofessional.com.

Mixed martial arts is by its nature a dangerous activity. Anyone practicing the techniques
in this book does so entirely at his or her own risk. Neither the publisher nor the authors
assume any responsibility whatsoever for any use or misuse of information appearing
anywhere in this book or for any injuries of any kind of any severity resulting from the
performance of the techniques contained herein. All images and text are for the purpose of
information only. Do not try anything in this book except under the direction of a physician
and under the full and vigilant supervision of a qualified instructor.

This book is printed on acid-free paper.

Contents

3 BASIC GROUND SKILLS: WRESTLING, PINS, ESCAPES, AND SUBMISSIONS   57

6   FULL MMA SPARRING AND COMPETITION   197

Introduction

The purpose of this book is to teach the sport of mixed martial arts (MMA), which involves boxing, kicking, striking, wrestling, and grappling, to fighters, both amateur and professional, and fans who want to get more out of the sport. People who want to add mixed martial arts to their training in a more specific art such as karate, aikido, Brazilian Jiu-Jitsu, judo, tae kwon do, wrestling, and so on, along with recreational athletes who do mixed martial arts to stay fit and happy and those who study mixed martial arts for self-defense purposes, will all get a lot out of this volume. While it aims to be complete, including a detailed section on the history of the game and extensive chapters describing and explaining skills, strategies, and fighting, minor moves and strategies are passed over to allow for focus on the most effective elements of this game. Also, only sport-specific topics are treated. Thus, generic weight lifting and endurance training regimens are left for fitness books to handle in more detail. Although the models wear T-shirts and shorts to make them easier to distinguish, this book is written for all forms of the sport, ranging from *gi* (wearing grappling jacket and pants) to no *gi* to shorts only, and from full to semi to light contact. However, due to all the myriad rule systems abounding in the world, we have taken the no *gi* full-contact form of this sport as its theoretical base for our purposes here.

This book was written to give you the skills and strategies you need to win in MMA, or, if you are a fan, to show you what the athletes are trying to do in the ring. By clearing away the unnecessary, we are left with a logical and coherent system of combat based on the nature of the human body and the potential that body has to overcome another. As trainers have repeated again and again through thousands of years, it is the basic, most efficient moves, performed by athletes who have developed high levels of stamina, power, and accuracy, that carry the day in the ring. The essence of mixed martial arts is high-energy simplicity in a complex environment. This book was written to help you achieve this aim, or if you are a fan, to understand how the athletes do it.

HISTORY AND ORIGINS

武
道

Most martial arts are mixed martial arts (MMA) in the sense that they mix together various skills. Styles known particularly for their striking also include grappling, and vice versa. For instance, karate, tae kwon do, and kung fu have throws, joint locks, and chokes, and Brazilian Jiu-Jitsu, judo, and sambo have punches, kicks, and so on. Some, like aikido, taekkyon, hapkido, and traditional Jiu-Jitsu, have always blended grappling almost evenly with striking. Even in the case of combat sports where either striking or grappling but not both is allowed, such as in wrestling, Kurash, or boxing, many athletes have been known to cross train. All martial arts have many important lessons to offer MMA fighters. Because MMA involves distinct phases of combat and several very different sets of skills, martial arts that focus on more specific aspects of fighting have a great deal to offer the mixed martial arts fighter in their areas of specialization. For example, Brazilian Jiu-Jitsu offers excellent submission techniques; judo teaches amazing throws and top game on the ground; wrestling covers awesome clinch and pinning skills; tae kwon do instructs fantastic kicks; Muay Thai deals devastating knees, feet, shins, and elbows; boxing specializes in killer punches; karate and kung fu develop skillful attacks of all kinds; and aikido, hapkido, and taekkyon have lots to share in mixing gripping and striking together. You can continue the list for every martial art there is.

Because of MMA's complexity, the specialization we see in the various martial arts is quite understandable. Besides, all martial arts were developed with specific fighting environments in mind, which in many cases include dealing with multiple opponents, weapons, clothing, and so on. Mixed martial arts demands excellent skills in all aspects of unarmed combat for a one-on-one competitive event. Style-versus-style matches have been going on ever since the dawn of time, with every generation believing that it was the first to think of the idea: wrestlers versus boxers; English (traditional) versus French (kicking) boxers; Italian rapier fencers versus German swordsmen; sumo wrestlers versus judoka; and so on. Alexander the Great even pitted a fully armed soldier against a top-notch MMA athlete. (The athlete won.) After thousands of years of this, we have a pretty good idea now of what works best in MMA competition.

The term *martial arts* is actually a direct translation of the Japanese concept of *budo*. The two words had rarely been put together in this way before in the English language. Prior to its coining, *combat sport* was used to describe things like boxing, fencing, and wrestling, while *military art* would refer to marksmanship, bayoneting, strategy, and tactics. "The art of self-defense" referred primarily to boxing, and "the gentle art" to wrestling. *Martial art*, the Japanese term, denotes a kind of activity that is not strictly speaking military but carries with it martial qualities: thus *martial* instead of *military* art. It is also not at its heart a sport, so *sport* could have nothing to do with the translation of the term. The martial arts were activities such as judo, karate, and kendo. The term has been extended in recent English usage to cover all fighting arts. The adding of *mixed* in front of *martial arts* was to label the kind of style-versus-style competition that garnered enormous international attention from the establishment of the Ultimate Fighting Championships in 1993 and Pride in 1997. It also sounds more refined than "all-out fighting," which is what the older Portuguese *vale tudo* and Greek *pankration* mean. Although intended at first to highlight the style-against-style nature of the fights, the "mixed" element of the name is now more broadly understood to refer to the complex linking of the distinct combat skills that this sport requires of its athletes in striking, controlling, and submitting an opponent. It really does look like a "mixed" sport, as sometimes flying knees to the head can be seen in the same fight as throws, pins, chokes, superman punches, and armlocks.

Unarmed martial arts were developed to handle situations where people without weapons had to defend themselves. Every society on earth developed unarmed combat systems. The accumulated experience in the science of unarmed fighting is terrifically old, going back to the dawn of time. Our focus in this chapter is on competitive systems of mixed martial arts around the world, the full-contact events through time. Due to the dangerous nature of mixed martial arts fights, only certain places at particular times allowed or promoted the sport, and our treatment therefore centers on them.

The Greeks

The first recorded MMA event we know about is the *pankration* in the Olympic Games of 648 B.C. Ancient writers tell us that it came about because people wanted to know who would win if a boxer fought a wrestler. The only prohibited techniques were gouging eyes, biting, and tearing the groin off. There were no rounds, and it was extremely popular. Although it sounds extreme, there is only one recorded death in the thousand years the *pankration* was enjoyed. The famous death occurred in the fifty-fourth Olympiad in 564 B.C. when one athlete had taken the other's back, got his hooks in, and was applying a rear naked choke. The fighter being choked, the two-time returning Olympic champion Arrichion, had trapped one of his antagonist's legs in a two-legs-on-one lock. Upon dying through strangulation, having refused to tap out, thinking his leglock would work, Arrichion's body relaxed and so shifted his weight that his opponent believed his own leg would snap. The opponent actually tapped out, and the dead athlete won! (The loser, having been beaten by a dead person, went into a long depression.) There is also the story of another fighter who, having lost the championship title seven times to the same rival, was preparing to finally defeat him in their eighth matchup. Unfortunately, his opponent died of an illness just before the Olympics started. Robbed of his chance to beat his rival and regain his honor, the fighter stood at the foot of the seven-time champion's statue at Olympia, cursing and swearing. Suddenly an earthquake shook all the land, and the statue toppled over and killed him. (You can decide for yourself if this second incident qualifies as a sport-related death or not.)

The *pankration*, while seen as more violent than wrestling, was thought much gentler than boxing, a fist-striking-only event with no gripping allowed, in which hard leather thongs were wrapped around the fists and forearms and sometimes dumbbells were held to increase the impact of punches. Puffy gloves like those used in modern boxing were worn only in training. Toughening the hands by striking speed and heavy bags was essential for boxers, and *pankratiasts* conditioned their feet in a similar fashion. Wrapping the hands with boxing thongs in *pankration* seems to have been optional, as some images depict them and others do not, but in boxing they were necessary.

One of the concerns many have had with MMA competitions regards the safety of the participants. Because of its great variety of effective tactics and moves, unexpected motions can result in more varied kinds of injuries than in more limited sports. In fact, because of its varied nature, no one part of the body is overly stressed in mixed martial arts, unlike in boxing where great care has to be taken to avoid injuring the brain through too many blows taken on the head, the main target of punches in that sport. In addition, most modern MMA rules have regulations maximizing the safety of the competitors. However, injury will always be a much loathed but unavoidable companion of this sport, as it is for every other sport.

The Romans

Roman enthusiasm for mixed martial arts, called *pancratium* in their Latin language, spread it throughout the Roman Empire's African, Asian, and European domains to 25 percent of the world's population at that time, and a vast array of different nationalities. Germans, Africans, Latins, Greeks, Arameans,

Jews, and others were united in this fierce and spectacular competitive sport. It became very popular all over the empire, and statues were raised to famous victors.

Unlike the gladiatorial combats, a form of often lethal submission fighting with weapons, where combatants were looked down on as slaves, the *pancratium* was a highly respected sport for the free citizens of the empire. There was no social stigma attached to it, and it was in fact seen as a highly cultured, elite activity. Under Roman law, *pancratiasts* and other combat athletes were exempt from military service, could organize into guilds, often taught as professors of the art, and were given special honors and distinctions. They were seen as examples of bravery and industry, the two primary Roman values, for the moral edification of all. The profession was thus a hybrid one of fighting, entertaining, and educating others. Children were sent to learn from *pancratium* professors as part of their regular education, citizen amateurs competed and trained in the public gymnasia and baths, wealthy people often had their own resident instructors, and everyone loved watching the public competitions in the circuses, hippodromes, theaters, and amphitheaters of the empire. There is evidence for female participation in the sport. The Roman Age was the greatest for MMA until very recent times.

Ancient sources describe and depict all the range of moves found in mixed martial arts events today. Images of rear naked choke attempts with hooks in from the bottom, top, and even standing are found all over the territory that Rome controlled. The guillotine choke is a common image too. Statues, paintings, and mosaics of athletes kicking and kneeing each other are just as plentiful. Armlocks and ground fighting scenes (including punching through the guard) are everywhere in appearance, perhaps best illustrated in the innumerable Greek vases and in Roman mosaics at Ostia and Tusculum. A common situation seen today, they were just as common back then, as was holding down and striking a turtling adversary. Takedowns being followed up with strikes are also common scenes in the artwork. One particularly spectacular finishing move is seen in one mosaic where victory is depicted through all three possible methods at once: choke, joint lock, and striking, all at the same time! The victim, who is turtling, is being strangled with the triangle choke from the top while his arm is being twisted back by one of his antagonist's hands, and he is being hit in the side of his head by his antagonist's other hand.

Philostratus, a Roman period writer, in his book *On Gymnastics*, explains that *pancratiasts* must make use of backward falls, which are not safe for use in wrestling, and grips in which victory can be obtained by falling down with the adversary. They must have skill in all kinds of strangling methods. They also wrestle with an opponent's ankle to achieve leglocks, and they twist his arm, besides hitting and jumping on him, only biting and gouging being prohibited. Submission could be indicated by voice, by raising the index finger of one hand, or by tap out. There is evidence for some tournaments specifically banning the grappling phase of *pancratium* in order to force the competitors to stay on their feet and kickbox with each other, although based on our sources it appears that kicking and striking with legs and arms were the predominant aspects of the sport regardless of the rules.

By the end of the imperial Roman era, enthusiasm for weaponry and full-contact chariot racing seems to have outweighed that for the traditional sports as gladiatorial combat, human versus animal fights, and extreme racing took center stage in the circuses and arenas of the empire. However, a new wave of humanism led to the banning of fights to the death, and the age of the medieval tournament was born. In medieval tourneys and combats, fought on horse and foot, one competed as part of a team or as an individual, until submission. A new prize system was introduced in some events where the loser had to pay the winner, rather than prizes being set aside beforehand. The winner could claim the loser's horse or armor as trophies or demand a sum of money. All manner of weaponry and grappling skills were employed. The horses were even taught to deliver kicks and to bite. Rather than mixed martial arts disappearing at this time, the concept was instead expanded to include weapons and even animals in ever more spectacular all-out fighting events, eagerly attended by enormous crowds!

Wrestling

Wrestling, which treats the most critical part of the MMA fight, the clinch, has been practiced in every culture around the world all through time. Generally looked upon as preparation for the battlefield, the rules vary very little from one nation to the next. The aim in all styles of wrestling is to knock the other person down to the ground and get on top of him or her. The reason for this is that in war, the one on the ground is normally helpless to weapon thrusts from the one on top, or from his or her comrades nearby. Some styles of wrestling demand touching the opponent's back to the ground, resulting in full loss of mobility for the loser; others only require any body part other than the feet to touch down. Even bending down could spell death in the melee, so some styles of wrestling such as the traditional French Greco-Roman style and Kurash do not allow leg grabs. In the context of MMA, where if trained properly the fists, elbows, knees, shins, and feet can become deadly weapons, the same logic applies as for the battlefield wrestling styles.

Submissions may or may not be allowed, depending on the style of wrestling. As standing submissions, even the standing guillotine choke, are quite difficult to apply against a skilled adversary, they tend to take second place to throws. On the ground submissions are easier to execute, but they tend to take second place to pins for those styles of wrestling whose rules permit ground fighting. All the world's wrestling styles prefer position over submission, and again, the mixed martial arts ring finds the same logic applicable. However, submissions have always been part of the game in one way or another. Victory in ancient Roman and Greek wrestling was achieved by touching the opponent's back to the ground or by submission. The emperor Nero committed suicide by asking his personal wrestling instructor to strangle him to death with the rear naked choke. This is an example of a mixed martial arts technique changing the course of history!

Wrestling plays a prominent part in the combat scenes in England's national epic *Beowulf.* Written in the Anglo-Saxon period and celebrating the ancestors of England's royal families, it describes wrestling as a crucial element of combat and a skill every warrior must have. Being "firm of foot," a wrestling trait, is described as one of the most important attributes of a hero. The first monster Beowulf slays is Grendel, and he defeats him with an armlock. As there is no tapping out in war, Beowulf tears Grendel's arm, including the shoulder joint, from his body and keeps it as a trophy to show to his friends. The monster later dies of his wounds. In the fight with Grendel's mother, Beowulf casts her to the ground, but she gets up before he can pin her. She then throws him down, and as he turtles up on all fours to stand up again, she presses down on his turtling frame and attempts to stab him in the back with her dagger. Fortunately Beowulf's sturdy chain mail armor protects him from the would-be lethal blow. He is able to escape the pin and get back to his feet, pick up a nearby sword lying on the ground, and cut his opponent's head off with it. "It was easy for the Ruler of Heaven to give him the victory when he got to his feet again," writes the poet (lines 1555–7).

In another book, *The Histories,* written in the same period by Procopius, a Byzantine Greek wrestling trainer named Bouzes faces a Persian foe in a one-on-one duel that starts on horseback and goes to the ground. After knocking the Persian off his horse with his lance, Bouzes has to dismount in order to pin and slit the throat of his adversary, most likely a very common requirement of ancient and medieval warfare. Next, a more experienced Persian soldier rides out to challenge him. The two charge at each other so furiously that their horses hit heads and are knocked out, sending both men falling to the ground. The wrestler's training is given as the reason for his being able to get up first from the ground after enduring the shock of the fall, take down and pin his opponent as he is getting up on one knee, and deliver a fatal stab. These examples are only the tip of the iceberg in terms of proof of how important wrestling skill was to success in war. It is easy to see why almost every culture on earth has its own version of the sport of wrestling. Fighters simply could not afford to neglect the art if they wanted their community to survive. It was this reasoning that drove Chinese emperors to select their bodyguards from winners in wrestling tournaments.

Boxing

Boxing is another crucial element of mixed martial arts. The fists are handily placed within easy reach of the opponent's head, and the head is the best target for strikes. These facts were discovered early on in history, far before written records, and the art of boxing began its immortal journey through the centuries. Lots of early documentation about the sport has survived from Greek and Roman times. In those days, fists and forearms were wrapped with tough leather bands of ox hide to protect the wearer and enable him or her to deal more devastating blows, much like modern mixed martial arts gloves. By ensuring the hands will not fracture, these bands allow the match to be a test of skill and stamina and not one of whose hands will break first or whose forearms will bleed more. Thus, the primary purpose of the gloves as described by ancient authors was to protect the hands and wrists from fracture and from breaking of the skin. The leather was also intended to cut the adversary. To make things more interesting, it became common in Roman times to hold dumbbells while boxing to add weight to the hits. The Romans also often sewed iron and lead strips or studs into the boxing gauntlets. In later times two metal knuckles often were made to protrude far out from the gauntlets. For training, round, padded gloves were worn, for all intents and purposes no different from modern boxing gloves. All these items were used by free citizens. Gladiators, the enslaved fighters, when ordered to box, were frequently given spikes to wear that were known to spill brains, a more lethal version of the protruding knuckles free fighters wore.

The Romans seem to have been enjoyed boxing, called *pugilatio* in Latin (now anglicized as *pugilism*), more than wrestling and were very much aware of its close affinity to armed combat. Boxing is the one combat sport that the Roman citizen Paul of Tarsus, writer of a large part of the Christian New Testament of the Bible, mentions: "so fight I, not as one that beateth the air" (1 Corinthians 9:26). Because of the use of hand-protecting gloves in today's martial arts competitions, the modern sport of MMA is as much like ancient *pugilatio* as it is like ancient *pancratium*. In the ancient *pancratium*, since wrestling, striking with other parts of the body than the fists, and grappling were all integral parts of the game, the wear and tear on the body was more evenly distributed over the entire frame, although the fact that the fists were still the major weapons is attested to by the wearing of boxing thongs by some *pancratiasts* in ancient mosaics and paintings. Boxing was as important a part of the ancient *pancratium* as it is for modern MMA fights. Competitors who fought in both events requested the boxing be held after the *pancratium* since it was a far more punishing event. Through the centuries boxing has been referred to as "fencing with the fists." There were no illegal punches or off-target areas in Greek and Roman boxing, and the groin was a common target, often resulting in submission. Victory was by submission through fatigue or severe beating, or by referee stoppage.

Nothing promoted boxing so much through the centuries as did the Roman national epic, later to become the pan-European epic, the *Aeneid*. For thousands of years the *Aeneid* stood as the best work of literature available in the Latin language, and having read it was a mark of proper education. It also brought, in great detail, the excitement and skills of the sport of boxing before the eyes of each succeeding generation of Westerners. The fighting scenes within the *Aeneid* read very much like a modern mixed martial arts match.

Boxing influenced the training of gladiators, whose methods in turn were used for the drilling of the legions of the Roman army. Instead of heavy and light punching bags, gladiators and soldiers attacked posts with sword and shield. Instead of in-club sparring bouts with soft, round, puffy gloves called *sphairai*, they engaged in fencing with wooden swords, sometimes ball-tipped, and wicker shields. Many emperors, including Augustus Caesar, the first emperor of Rome, were avid fans, patrons, and practitioners of boxing.

Medieval documents, such as lists of injuries and their causes in a given area, legal records, and period literature, prove boxing's continued popularity, along with all the other ancient sports, through the Middle Ages. Towns, cities, and even small villages held regular athletic contests. Priests were known to teach the art of boxing to youth in order to encourage them to defend their honor with fists rather than with swords. It is of salient importance for the history of MMA to point out that in the Middle Ages, and until the advent of the Marquess of Queensberry rules in nineteenth-century England, "boxing" permitted wrestling holds, and striking was allowed to continue on the ground, making it actually more a kind of mixed martial arts competition than what the Greeks and Romans or modern people would consider boxing to be. Even biting was sometimes permitted. Medieval knights were expected to train heavily in boxing and wrestling to develop toughness and combat skills, and it was something of a proverb of the time that unless you had some of your teeth knocked out, you were not yet a true knight. Kickboxing was also popular, especially in France, where the competitors wore stiff shoes called *savates* and were not permitted to use the hands except to block with.

John "Jack" Broughton (1703–1789) was the founder of modern boxing. He was a champion boxer and rower and also a personal bodyguard of the English king George II, alongside whom he fought in the Battle of Dettingen. Broughton opened up an amphitheater where he held fights with weapons, boxing matches, and also animal combats of various kinds in the tradition of the Roman gladiatorial events. Due to Broughton's enthusiasm for and promotion of the sport, boxing took on the status of the national combat sport of the English-speaking world, as it had been for the Romans more than a thousand years earlier. His rules were the major inspiration for the formalized Marquess of Queensberry rules that became the standard rules of boxing starting in 1867. The use of gloves to protect the fists in modern MMA is due more than anything else to the expectation of fans accustomed to watching professional boxing to see its techniques performed in the ring. The division of mixed martial arts fights into rounds, the scoring of striking techniques higher than grappling ones when the fight goes to the judges' decision, and the practice of requiring competitors engaged in very slow ground grappling to stand are all due to a culture imbued with the rules and skills of boxing and love of the sport.

Muay Thai

In spite of the importance of the fists in mixed martial arts competitions, and in spite of the fact that boxing has always been a full-contact event, MMA requires more than just the fists to strike with. Thailand has a tradition of mixed martial arts events going back to the earliest records. While boxing is arguably the national combat sport of the English-speaking world, Muay Thai is without dispute the national sport of Thailand. There is even a Muay Thai Day celebrated on March 17 in honor of the sport and its place in Thailand's national culture and history. Muay Thai is unique among historical full-contact sports due to a combination of several factors: the laxity of its rules, the length of time it has been practiced, and its enormous popularity throughout the millennia since its inception. Unlike the Roman *pancratium*, Muay Thai did not lose its popularity to other events; it has remained strong right up until today. It is thus the greatest example of a living, full-contact, mixed martial arts tradition. Modern kickboxing and the mixed martial arts style shoot boxing, both originating in Japan in the twentieth century, were inspired by it.

Nearby countries also practice the sport but under different names and sometimes with more extreme rules. The Burmese *Lethwei* traditionally had no rules at all. Even biting was allowed. A knocked-out competitor was asked upon revival if he wished to continue the fight. Only the acknowledged submission of the adversary enabled a competitor to win. An adversary's simply refusing to submit no matter what occurred, including death, would result in a draw.

Muay Thai traditionally allowed striking with any part of the body. This meant that fists, elbows, knees, shins, feet, and the head were all used. Grappling was also allowed and was used for holding the opponent to deliver strikes and to slam the opponent to the ground. No part of the body was off-limits to attack, and some fighters specialized in striking the groin with the knee, foot, or other parts. Kicks were often aimed at the knee of the opponent's supporting leg in order to break it. As Muay Thai evolved as an art with military application just as wrestling styles did, the prohibition against continuing the fight on the ground is understandable. Fists were often wrapped in sturdy rope, and adding sharp materials to the rope was not unknown. Victory was attained by beating the adversary to such a degree that he could not continue the match. Thus, developing toughness was a key element in training. In more recent times the rules have been altered in favor of protecting the competitors more. Points are now tallied, head butts and groin strikes prohibited, and modern boxing gloves worn.

From Judo to Brazilian Jiu-Jitsu

Starting in the early twentieth century, mixed martial arts events were held in Brazil, referred to as *vale tudo* competitions. These events permitted all standing and ground techniques just like the ancient *pancratium* did. This competitive environment attracted the attention of some Brazilian judo schools, which began to adapt judo to this kind of "anything goes" event. Judo began in Japan in the late nineteenth century as a form of full-contact grappling wearing garments that represent street wear, called *judogis,* in order to replicate real-world fighting conditions, which typically involved clothed individuals.

Judo combined the fighting specialties of several very old fighting traditions into one all-inclusive grappling sport. Much like other forms of wrestling, and for the same combative reasons, judo aims to throw to the back, pin, or submit an opponent. The separate origins of the two major parts of judo are still visible today, as throwing and ground grappling are normally practiced distinctly from one another and are kept as two exclusive forms of sparring, known as *standing randori* and *newaza randori,* or more commonly simply as *randori* and *newaza,* respectively. In addition, the weapon self-defense and striking techniques are kept quite apart from these two major parts.

The Brazilian stylists began to develop a fighting doctrine based on the *vale tudo* rules, where knocking the opponent out or making the opponent submit in a one-on-one fight is paramount. Thus, the throws and pins, which are dominant but not final actions in and of themselves in a full-out fight, were reduced in value from match-enders to point-scorers. The real challenge became achieving the submission, while winning on points from the throws and pins was a secondary objective. The rules of judo were also altered to promote a strategy centered on gaining the submission by progressing through several positions toward maximum control of the opponent. Thus, the ideal progression is to take down the adversary with a throw; pass the guard; establish a side control such as a side mount, scarf hold, or knee on belly pin; and from there achieve full mount. From this pin the opponent can be punched at will, mercilessly, with both hands and submitted with a vast array of locks and chokes. If the adversary turns over to his belly to escape the blows and submission attempts, one is then able to take his back by wrapping the heels tightly into the inner thigh area by the groin and snaking the arms around the neck for a choke hold. Taking the back in this way became a point-scoring move in these new rules. It is then possible to stretch the opponent's body out by pressing in with the hips and pulling back with the arms and legs, making the opponent totally helpless to strangulation.

This Brazilian form of judo has become known as Brazilian Jiu-Jitsu (BJJ) and is a unique example of a grappling art whose rules were designed expressly for the mixed martial arts arena. There are two subdivisions of the sport, one that continues to use the *judogi*, also called a kimono, as an approximation of street clothing better adapted for self-defense training purposes, and another more specific to mixed martial arts that is done without the *judogi*, often called submission grappling, no *gi* grappling, or just grappling. Since the *gi* has been proven a liability rather than a help in MMA combat, training without it more directly prepares one for the kind of grappling situation to be expected in the mixed martial arts ring.

Judo as a sporting form of self-defense training has evolved somewhat in the opposite direction in favor of dominating in the clinch position through throws. For MMA, judo throws are adapted to no *gi* wrestling grips. Freestyle and Greco-Roman wrestling have always been seen as the no *gi* counterparts to judo, so the creation of a specifically no *gi* variant of judo was not necessary.

While it is an oversimplification, it can be helpful when thinking of mixed martial arts to think of its techniques as encompassing all those found in boxing, kickboxing, Muay Thai, wrestling, and grappling. By no means are these the only sources for MMA competitors developing skills and tactics for the arena, but these are the most time-tested full-contact combat sports, including of course their many modern derivatives as legitimate subdivisions. Combining all these seemingly distinct sets of skills into one art is what makes mixed martial arts such a challenging field of endeavor, but also so interesting.

It would be beyond the scope of this book to go into any more detail about the full history of mixed martial arts around the world. The description in this chapter is only intended to show the documented antiquity of the sport and its greatest periods, and thereby properly dignify it with the age and tradition it has rightfully earned. Today's MMA competitors stand in the same noble tradition as their ancient forebears. Many still represent the threefold nature of the profession as competitors, entertainers, and teachers, and they continue to most excellently display the epitome of athleticism and courage combined in this most demanding of all combat sports.

BASIC SKILLS:
STRIKING AND DEFENSE

武
道

A lot of training is done alone, whether in total solitude or under the watchful eye of your coaches. There are several objectives you are looking to accomplish with your solo training regimen. You are seeking to develop strength and speed so that you can overpower and outpace your adversaries. You also need to improve your stamina so you can outlast all challengers. Physically you are looking to build muscle mass, bone density, and cardiovascular capacity. Mentally you must drill the fighting patterns into your memory so that the commands fire as quickly as possible through the neuron paths in your brain, without any delay.

Solo Training

There are three attributes in particular that you must develop as much as possible while solo training. The first is *power*, which is the combination of speed and strength. Plyometric exercises like leaping and jumping are excellent for this. Punching and striking are plyometric by their very nature.

The second attribute is *stamina*. Mixed martial arts is essentially about making the opponent tire out before you do so you are at an advantage in dealing devastating moves. Hitting your opponent tires him or her out, but opponents can be their own worst adversaries by tiring themselves out for you or by not being fit enough to last in the ring.

The third attribute is *accuracy*, which is extremely important. It is one thing to hit a bag that does not move around or retaliate, but it is another to hit a living, breathing target that fights back. Being able to, in the heat of the moment, not only make contact with your opponent, but actually deal maximum damage is the most difficult part of mixed martial arts, particularly so in this sport because mere touching does not count for points. Not only that, but in mixed martial arts, unlike in any more restrictive combat game, your opponent could be almost anywhere relative to you, including flying through the air, underneath you, spinning around, on top of you, and so on. Being able to hit accurately and with full power in such a varied fighting environment, while having to worry about grappling holds as well, is what makes mixed martial arts such an extremely difficult sport to become even moderately proficient at.

The accuracy attribute also refers to wrestling holds and grappling moves. The subtlest differences in grip, body position, and balance can make the exact same move either work spectacularly or fail miserably. Endless wrestling practice, sparring, striking moving focus pads at full speed from all different angles, grappling on the ground, mixed sparring where you put everything together, all must be done to the maximum. Isolate and then combine skills. Practice boxing, which involves your main weapons in MMA, your fists. Do kickboxing, wrestling, and submission grappling; then combine standing striking and grappling, ground grappling and boxing, transitional fighting in the clinch. Isolate and combine, isolate and combine!

There are a number of standard ways to develop the fundamental skills and strengths. They are running and jogging, jumping rope, weight training, and hitting the speed and heavy bags. There are also irregular methods that vary from coach to coach and from competitor to competitor, such as dragging heavy weights around, hitting tires with a sledge hammer, and so on. This book covers the standard methods and gives you a taste of some irregular ones too.

RUNNING AND JOGGING

Running is common to training in almost all sports. It is a natural movement for the body and strengthens nearly every muscle group. It also develops the heart, lungs, and both mental and physical endurance. In terms of mixed martial arts, it trains you to lunge forward at your opponent and to keep your balance while moving. To make running and jogging more sport specific, it is advisable to shadowbox with your arms while chugging along with your legs. This is a significantly more demanding workout because you have to keep your arms up and punching instead of following their natural swinging pendulum motions. Often bring the knees up too, as if kneeing an adversary or blocking kicks. It is a good idea to jog on the spot while punching the speed bag or heavy bag, the "jog and jab." This exercise closely mimics the kinds of motions and shifting of balance that occur in real competition. Walking is a healthy and gentle exercise for your body and is used to complement the more intense running and jogging.

JUMPING AND SKIPPING

Jumping rope is a critical part of fight training. In the ring, you have to stay on the balls of your feet in order to ensure speedy mobility. If you are flat-footed, you cannot move quickly. Skipping gives your feet and legs the endurance training they need to keep you on your toes throughout the match. It develops the explosive blast-off power and speed you require to deliver explosive strikes and throws. It makes your whole body tough, rugged, and strong, as it is a short jarring motion repeated over and over again, sending shock waves throughout your entire frame. The osteoblast film covering your bones is shaken by this, and it sends signals out to your brain that it needs to build more bone mass. The brain replies by sending calcium and other nutrients to make your bones stronger. Jumping thereby develops toughness and bone solidity throughout your entire body. By jumping up and down you perfect your balance, and by swinging the rope under your feet you improve your reaction time and awareness as well as strengthen the muscles in your arms and shoulders. Your fists get stronger for punching and so does your grip for grappling. Your legs get stronger for kicks. Jumping is a fantastic cardiovascular exercise too. It relates closely to the delivery of flying techniques in combat such as the flying knee and flying superman punch. It even helps in achieving certain kinds of guard passes and maintaining top position on the ground. Jumping can be done without the rope too. Jumping and punching, the "jump and jab," can be done on the bags or in the air, as can jumping and kneeing and so on. Leaping forward at the bag, delivering a strike, and then jumping back again is the lateral variant of this and even more accurately mimics the forward and backward motions you need to use in the ring.

WEIGHT LIFTING

Weight training is an important part of your training. Without weights you can do squats, push-ups, and sit-ups. Any weight-bearing exercise, like jumping or running, is by its nature a form of weight training. Wrestling is a form of live one-on-one weight training. With weights and other equipment you can do everything else too. Punching while holding light weights can help with stamina. A weighted rope helps make skipping better for your upper body. You have to gear your weight-training regimen to your body and your particular needs and goals. A whole book in itself could be written on this topic, and much of it is outside the sport-specific scope of this book.

EQUIPPING YOUR GYM

To train effectively you need equipment. Logistically this is as important a part of your training strategy as the drills you dedicate your time toward mastering. You need wrestling or judo mats to practice wrestling and grappling skills and crash mats for repeating throws. A full-sized ring or cage similar to what you expect to fight in is basically a must if you want to fight professionally: you need to learn how the space and composition will affect your movement. Boxing gloves, hand wraps, headgear, and focus mitts and pads are all needed for striking practice and sparring. Heavy and speed bags along with bag mitts are all good investments. Skipping ropes, light, weighted, or heavy, and light dumbbells are all good for your jumping exercises. Free weights and/or weight lifting devices are needed for grip and body strength development. Climbing ropes are also good.

A running track, or at least a designated running area inside the gym, allows you to run without having to be concerned about what the weather is doing outside. A mouth guard is necessary to help protect your teeth—preferably one made by your dentist. A steel groin cup is needed as well. MMA gloves cannot be done without. Shin pads are needed for kicking sparring. Kicking pads and shields and body guards are all good to have too.

More than anything you need one or more dedicated coaches and training partners. The better the people you work with, the better a fighter you will be. Often having several specialist coaches who are experts in their chosen full-power combat sport is a very good idea. Thus, having a submission grappling or Brazilian Jiu-Jitsu coach, a wrestling or judo coach, and a kickboxing or Muay Thai coach who is good at both free and clinch striking is quite sensible. Added to this you might choose to have a designated boxing coach or a tae kwon do or similar kicking-devoted art coach to provide focus for you on those specific ranges of combat. Who you are working with is even more important than what equipment you are working with. You need all of these things if you are thinking of going professional with your MMA.

If you are instead primarily interested in mixed martial arts for recreational, self-defense, or amateur sport purposes, you can get away with less equipment. If you are interested in using your MMA skills for self-defense, then you should invest in a *gi* and do at least some of your training in it, as it approximates clothing that people wear in everyday life. The *gi* changes the gripping strategies somewhat. If your goal is to participate in amateur mixed martial arts, then you need to be familiar with the rules of your league. Certain techniques described in this book, such as knees and elbows or striking below the belt, might be limited or banned for safety reasons from amateur competitions. You might not be allowed to hit full power, changing the emphasis of your striking training from power and accuracy to speed and accuracy—even changing the kind of techniques you might choose to employ. Also, more safety gear might be required, and certain equipment standards might be expected before you can participate. Check with your association to find out exactly what the rules are and what you have to wear into the competition.

EFFICIENT MOVEMENT

Keep in mind though that power is not bulk dependent. Power is more a matter of how fast you can move. The speed you deliver your techniques at is not only dependent on your whole body working together, your overall fitness, and how well trained your neurons are for them, but also on how efficiently you have learned to perform them. Exactly what is the most efficient way to do any given move depends a lot on your precise body shape and composition. The more you practice your moves, the clearer it will be to you what the fastest ways are to do them. This brings up a kind of interesting paradox where it is your body that teaches your mind about how it wants to move naturally, and your mind follows the body's advice. The best fighters say that they learn to improve their technique, to make it more efficient, only when they are completely exhausted, when they have to rely on precise and efficient motions, not on strength or stamina. Therefore, make sure you achieve this state of fatigue in your training so as to learn from your body how it wants to move with the least muscular effort required. Allow your body to teach you. Your own body is your best teacher. No book or coach, no matter how good, can teach you what only your own unique body can.

STRETCHING

Flexibility needs to be mentioned as it is an important trait that keeps the body supple and minimizes certain kinds of training injuries related to stiffness. Rotating the shoulders is very important to keep them supple. Stretching the legs is vital to improve the speed and range of kicks. All the standard stretches like the splits, touching toes, and so on, are advisable in order to reduce tightness in the back, groin, quads, hamstrings, shoulders, neck, and even wrists and fingers.

DRILLING

Of course, practicing striking techniques and other movements alone and in combinations is all part and parcel of training. Hitting speed and heavy bags with fists, elbows, knees, shins, and feet is necessary, as are drilling and shadowboxing with all these same weapons. There is also something to be said for holding light dumbbells sometimes while drilling striking techniques, since this kind of added resistance training can increase your stamina for keeping your arms up during the match and improve your grip strength. However, the dumbbells slow you down, so unless they are precisely the weight of your MMA gloves, they can be a bad thing if overdone.

Throwing a wrestling dummy around is also a good idea, as is pinning a heavy bag on the floor in full or side mount (more on these in the next chapter), north-south, knee on belly, or even a scarf hold, and hitting it with all manner of hammer fists, punches, elbows, and knees. Getting a coach to hold focus mitts for you is always a good idea too. All of these drilling activities will eventually lead you to sparring, which, regardless of the specifics, is one of the most indispensable components of your training.

OTHER TYPES OF TRAINING

Isometric deep stance training combined with striking or blocking movements can produce strong legs and can add stability and rigidity to kicks. At the same time it isolates the arms and torso and develops flexibility and power for bashing and blocking. It can also provide a happy change from the more jarring exercises in your regimen such as skipping, hitting the bags, and running as it exercises your body differently. Deep lunges relate closely to many fighting moves.

Originally from karate and kung fu, deep stances such as the horse stance and front stance are found useful by some MMA athletes, full-contact karateka, and kickboxers. The horse stance is adopted by placing the feet parallel on the floor about double shoulder width apart and flexing the knees somewhat. Pressure is felt to push outward through the edges of the feet. The front stance is formed by first pivoting the feet on the heels from the horse stance at least 45 degrees. Then the front knee is bent and the back knee straightened rigidly. It must be emphasized that these stances are employed for conditioning purposes and are not fighting stances for the ring.

Rolling to the ground from your feet and back up to them again at all different angles is an important safety skill for when you fall or are forced down to the floor. Being able to get up again is very important. Mixing sprawling (jumping your feet back and falling forward onto your palms to avoid a leg grab takedown) in with your shadowboxing, or with your jogging or jumping, also falls into this category of controlled falling training. Cartwheels come in handy sometimes too.

Climbing rope is good for your grappling muscles, as is climbing rocks. Playing catch with a medicine ball is good as a form of plyometrics, similar to doing clapping push-ups. Playing soccer can certainly help with delivering kicks and knees, including flying techniques. Manual labor activities such as carrying heavy loads, dragging things, bashing and hammering things, digging holes, and other physical pursuits can be a form of training. On the more extreme end of things, dancing around in a circle while staring at a finger to improve focus in combat, throwing a fallen tree and then running to throw it again, and even boxing with kangaroos are exercises known to have been employed by some combat athletes.

Basics

Mixed martial arts requires that you turn your entire body into a battery of weapons. MMA fighting follows the principles of war: you are trying to catch your opponent at an unexpected time. Usually the technique itself is not unexpected, as most serious MMA fighters know the moves that are used in the sport. It is only with proper timing that you can trick your adversary and gain an advantage. It is the fact that your opponent is not expecting the move at that particular time that makes it work, or he or she might expect it too late to effectively defend against it. In Chapter 4, where we set up effective strategies, preparing surprises is at the heart of it. In this chapter and the next we cover the basic separate elements of combat. Here is where we start to get technical.

There is no perfect way to do any technique that applies to all people, since everyone's body is different and the complexities of the fight mean that every move has to be adjusted to work at the time. So exactly how you angle a punch, for example, will depend on where your opponent's face is or is heading at that moment. There are some basic principles. One of them is speed. You have to be fast. Fighting is fast. This goes for the grappling aspects too. You have to hit fast, throw fast, pin fast, submit fast. Be explosive! You need to be strong too, but never forget that you have to be quick as lightning. Speed increases force, as the physicists tell us. So work to get *fast*! Fast punches hurt, slow ones do not. Fast submissions get the tap out, slow ones are escaped. Think about it.

When you hit your adversary, your real goal is not to score a knockout or injury right away, even though it would be nice to do so. What hitting is really about is wearing down your opponent's body. The effect is similar to your opponent getting tired out, but the beating he or she is receiving from you everywhere accelerates the process. Forcing your opponent to keep his or her arms up in a boxing stance is another way to tire your adversary out, so even if you are not at first able to land many blows, you might be able to later on when your opponent has grown weary. Getting bashed and smashed over and over makes the muscles slower to react and harder to move. Joints begin refusing to cooperate. Sore muscles put more strain on the lungs and heart. An opponent who has received punches to the head stops thinking tactically. Eventually your adversary will end up being vulnerable due to exhaustion, and at this point you can pounce in for the kill with your knockout blows or submission techniques.

Take for example getting kicked in the thigh with a roundhouse kick. It hurts the first time. After the thirtieth time the recipient of the kicks will not be able to walk anymore or use his leg for anything else in the match either. Matches have gone like this, where the victim of repeated strikes like the roundhouse kick eventually collapses onto the floor like a felled tree. But this is not to say that you cannot get lucky early in the match with a knockout or winning strike or a quick submission. If you win quickly, all the best, but be ready to go the distance. When you read about the moves, you must consider what effect they have on hurting or exhausting your opponent. Hurting and exhausting your opponent are the two keys to victory. The final strikes and submissions are like opening the now unlocked door. Think about this.

Your main defense is good cardiovascular endurance, as the fighter who tires first usually loses. In fact, stamina is the most important single element in mixed martial arts competition. No matter how good your techniques are, if you get tired you will lose. And even if you are a bit less skilled than your adversary, if you can outlast his or her stamina, you can win.

THE FIGHTING STANCE

The fighting stance is not a precise thing, and it varies a lot in the match. You will find it convenient to stand with your feet about shoulder width or more apart and one foot in front of the other.

The Fighting Stance

The Feet in the Fighting Stance

Exactly how you angle your feet is up to you, and their angles will change depending on what is going on in the match. Keep the front one almost but not quite pointed at your adversary so that you are facing him and not turning your back. This front foot will angle inward a bit, roughly at 30 degrees, which is not much. Angling it like this is for comfort, since forcing your foot to remain twisted directly at your opponent unnaturally strains your leg and prevents easy movement: your feet naturally like to be close to parallel with each other rather than splayed outward. Your back foot will tend to angle outward. You are on the balls of both feet in order to utilize the springiness of your instep to snap around the floor. Your stance will appear like a fencer about to stab someone with your lead arm, and this makes sense since lunging forward is a major part of most attacks.

You will probably prefer keeping the same positioning most of the time, with a regular lead and back foot. Because keeping the left foot forward and the right back is more common, we describe the techniques in the book using this orthodox stance, although we use the designations "front" and "back" as much as possible for the sake of southpaw readers. When you have the other foot in front, as you often will, or if you prefer your right in front most of the time, simply reverse the "right" and "left" designations in your mind. Many people like to keep their more coordinated and stronger side back from the opponent, since it is the side that has more windup space to inflict damage. When you are hitting your adversary with your best weapons, you want maximum accuracy and power. Still, some prefer their more dextrous side in front so as to more handily entrap and grapple with the opponent. Being close to ambidextrous as far as fighting skill goes is certainly a desired thing in mixed martial arts so that your opponent has to deal with attacks from all sides. Keep your right fist outside your face and your left fist forward in front of your face and outside.

Hands Up (Front View)

Hands Up (Side View)

Do not splay your elbows out, but rather keep them in enough to allow your arms to block attacks.

Be ready to raise your knees to defend against kicks.

BASIC PRINCIPLES OF DEFENSE

Your defense against striking relies mostly on slight adjustments in your on guard position and in raising your legs up against kicks. Think of your forearms, elbows, knees, and shins as shields. If you need good coverage against a strong attack on one side, raise that side's knee up and set your elbow slightly outside it, building a big shield out of the meeting of your arm and leg on that side.

You can block kicks and strikes to the outside or to the inside with your shield, depending on where they are coming from and what is best for you at the moment. It is helpful to add your other hand into this shield, making it a veritable fortress. But be careful about getting thrown down, or about get-

Shin and Arm Blocking Same-Side Kick   **Kicking Out the Supporting Leg**

ting your supporting leg kicked. It is common sense when one of the opponent's legs is raised in the air to kick across into the other one.

Do not bob and weave too much either, as doing so makes you liable to get kneed, kicked in the head, or pushed into the ground. You should know how to bob and weave as it can certainly come in handy in a match, but do not expect to do it anywhere near as much as a boxer would in a boxing fight.

Be ready to sprawl to defend against the double leg takedown. A slight movement backward or to one side or the other is more often than not an effective defense against most striking attacks.

Retreating all around the ring is no way to be a mixed martial arts fighter, but tactically moving backward and forward makes a lot of sense in terms of efficiently dealing with attacks and dealing back retaliation.

BASIC GOALS OF WRESTLING

Blocking quickly turns into wrestling as both you and your opponent try to control each other's body. Wrestling on your feet might last only an instant with a few grips leading to more strikes, or it might go on for a while, mixed with knees, elbows, and punches, and end up in a throw to the ground. While wrestling with your adversary, there are several scientifically proven tricks to gain the upper hand. One is to snake one of your hands around behind your opponent's head and punch or elbow his face with your other hand. This is the *single overhook*.

Another is the *double overhook*, where you snake both hands over your opponent's shoulders and tightly clasp them together behind his head, squeezing the neck with your forearms.

Do not interlace your fingers though, as this is weak. Rather, place one hand over the other. Try to pull your adversary's head

Single Overhook

Double Overhook

down, dragging him around and keeping him off balance, and deliver a lot of knees into his face with glee. If you take a tight squeezing hold with both hands under your adversary's shoulders around the back, called the *double underhook*, you can stop an overhook attack on yourself and set up throws like the back throw, hip throw, and leg hook throws.

The shoulder throw, a special technique that depends on speed, uses a very particular starting grip on the wrist and biceps under the shoulder (this grip is shown in Chapter 3).

The *over-under grip* is achieved with one arm over the shoulder on one side and the other arm under the shoulder on the other side, gripping tightly around the back.

This grip is quite common because it is equal for both fighters, and they are often content to fight from it, allowing each

Double Underhook
Fighter on the left takes the double underhook.

Over-Under
Fighter on the right lifts his opponent off balance with the over-under.

other to keep the grip for a time because it gives neither fighter an advantage or a disadvantage. Lots of throws are done from the over-under grip. Some throws, like the double leg, do not depend on any kind of starting grip. The single leg throw can be done after trapping a kicking or blocking leg, or more aggressively, just going in for it while wrestling. Always be careful though about crouching down to grab your opponent's legs since you could eat knees and kicks. When on the ground, the main thing is to stay on top, but more on that in its proper place. You have to be able to wrestle in the clinch. If you cannot prevent takedowns, you cannot win. No matter how good a striker you are, if you can be taken down at will, you cannot use your striking moves to any good effect. And no matter how good a grappler you are, if you are taken down and end up on the bottom every time, you are going to have a very hard time of it. Wrestling in the clinch can be said to be the foundation of MMA fighting. Wrestling and grappling skills are dealt with in full detail in Chapter 3.

STRIKING TECHNIQUES

Of all striking techniques, the most important are the punches. The reason for this is physiological. Your arms are free to move around in the air, whereas your legs are needed to keep your body from falling over. The farther you can hit, the better, so the fist is the more useful part of your arm to strike with in the complexities of a match. Even though the elbow is a more powerful weapon than the fist, it only has half the range of the fist. Although the knees and legs are far more powerful than the elbow even, they are occupied most of the time with keeping your body up and moving around. So even though of the list of useful striking points the fists are the weakest, they are the most convenient to use, have a rather long range, are still very powerful, and happen to be located high on your body so as to be able to better reach your opponent's face and head. The face and head are the most vulnerable parts of the body to strike, due to the weakness of the neck and each fighter's need to protect himself against a possible concussion. Having indicated all this, every striking technique described here is important in MMA. Knockouts can be scored with any of them. They all wear down your opponent. All have their uses.

Cross. This is the most important single strike in MMA. Since you actually have to hurt your opponent, not just score lots of touches with your front hand, this punch reigns supreme among punching attacks. The traditional name for this punch is the *cross punch*, since the punch travels across your body from behind to in front. Crossing over is what gives it its power, and it is known as MMA's power punch. Another name for the cross is the *reverse*.

From the orthodox, left foot in front stance described above, the right fist is used to deliver this devastating blow. It travels

Cross

straight out from where you are keeping it next to your face into your opponent's face, from face to face in the blink of an eye—ideally putting as much of a smile on the thrower's face as it takes away from the recipient. Your palm turns to face down. Rotate your right shoulder forward and shrug it up to keep your face covered in case of a counterstrike. Twist your right hip forward too, as far as you can. Lunge forward with your left foot and allow your right to angle up on the ball of the foot, also rotating into the attack.

The punch is stronger if you have the feeling of grinding into the ground with your rear foot, but this is not to say that the cross cannot be done with your back foot travelling through the air. If your body is moving forward, you can still land a heavy punch with your back foot up.

Even though rotation is involved, think of the punch as a linear thing, aimed directly at the target. Surely a moving target will require creative angles of delivery, but always think of the move as a direct stab into the victim as if your knuckles had blades jutting out from them. Deliver the punch with the area of the first two knuckles. Hitting any part of the face or jaw is excellent as these parts of the head are weak. You can of course aim to hit the solar plexus, ribs, and other vulnerable parts of the torso too. The main target, though, is the head because it is easier to hit. If you fly through the air to deliver this or any other punch, it is called a superman punch. All striking techniques can be delivered with a jump. Remember to train to deliver them *fast* and with *accuracy*!

To deliver the most effective strike, you need to keep your fists strong through good hand strength–building exercises involving gripping including any weight lifting activity, climbing, skipping rope, grappling, hitting the bag, punching with weights, and so on. Good strong hand muscles make your fists less likely to get injured in training and competition and make your punches harder and even heavier. We do not use big puffy gloves in MMA. Although we do use small gloves, the hand itself needs to be strong.

On the ground, if you are in your opponent's guard, you can try to punch to the face, combining punches with hammer fists. If you can get up on your feet into a wide stance, you can develop a lot of rotational motion using your legs and torso to wind into your punches. As your adversary is worried about getting his face knocked in, you can step or hop around or through his legs and get to a better position such as full mount or side mount. (More on them later.)

Jab. Even though the cross punch is about 30 percent more powerful than the jab, the jab is extremely important due to its greater range of motion, and it is in fact the second most important technique in MMA. Because the jab is delivered with your lead hand and therefore closer to your opponent, you can send it more quickly and have a much better chance of making contact. It can also work as a distraction by blocking your adversary's vision, as it is normally launched at the face. It can also function in blocking as a shield against punches and as a push to keep distance between your opponent and you, either by stopping your adversary's advance, knocking him backward, or helping you to push off backward away from your opponent with the help of your legs. You can knock an opponent out with it; it is a strong punch when delivered with proper attitude. The main thing to keep in mind is that in MMA actually hurting your adversary matters, so focus on making your jabs both speedy and powerful.

The jab is delivered by shooting your lead fist straight out from your on guard position at your opponent's face, and sometimes other targets depending on the circumstances. Your shoulder shrugs up to cover your face, and you also rotate your shoulder and hip forward to achieve maximum extension. You lunge forward with your same-side foot. Thus, if you are jabbing

Jab

with your left hand, you lunge with your left foot. When you have disturbed your opponent's balance, motion, distance, stance, or vision with a jab or two or three, then you can make an attempt to score a cross punch. It is particularly deceptive if you feel comfortable fighting with either your right or left foot forward so that you can keep a constant painful bombardment of punches coming at your adversary while advancing forward. When the side that your adversary expects to be jabbing turns into the cross punch and vice versa, your hits become harder to avoid. If you jump and jab, it becomes a superman punch just like the cross punch does, benefiting from the extra force supplied by the jump. Inside your opponent's guard you should try to stand up in a wide and balanced stance and deliver punches from both fists into your adversary's face.

Hook. The hook is a modification of the preceding punches, made to hit a close target. No matter which hand you are hitting with, the movement is the same. You get your elbow up so that your forearm is parallel with the floor, and you punch directly at the target while pivoting strongly with your same-side foot, hip, and shoulder. A picture-perfect hook supposedly has a 45-degree angle at the elbow. As with the other punches, shrug your shoulder up for defense. You do not necessarily need to rotate your palm down. You can keep it perpendicular to the ground and facing you if you wish or the situation dictates. This is a really great punch when you have come to grips. Combining it with the single overhook grab with the other hand is an awesome technique. If you jump and rotate in the air while executing this technique, it can surprise and intimidate your adversary.

Hook

Uppercut. The uppercut is used to strike upward from below. It is a good way to slip through the space between someone's parallel forearms in the on guard position and deliver contact to the chin. You start the punch low and angle it straight up at the target. In MMA it is best not to crouch down much while dealing the uppercut because of the danger of knees and wrestling holds. Move your body as you would for a jab or cross punch: if your lead hand throws the uppercut, the rest of your body moves as for the jab; if your back hand throws it, move as you would for the powerful cross punch. You can make this punch a flying technique just like the others by jumping through the air to deliver it.

Spinning Backfist. This strike is nearly as strong as the cross punch. You deliver it with the hand that is farthest back. Your back leg, let us say left leg, spins your whole body around clockwise, pivoting on your forward right foot. Your left fist spins

Uppercut

Spinning Backfist

around with it, generating momentum, and hits home on your opponent's face with great force.

Be sure to turn your head a little before your body so that you see your target clearly and aim before your hand gets there. The spinning backfist is a very showy move but can be risky, as you have to turn your back to make it work. It is therefore a less common move, although it does score sometimes. It is good to use to confuse your opponent, as it is an attack that does everything the opposite of what is to be expected. Just make sure you do not end up confusing yourself instead!

Hammer Fist. This is also known as the rabbit punch, but "hammer fist" sounds tougher than anything to do with bunnies. You raise your fist up and strike down on your adversary's head, face, or other target. If you are delivering this punch on your feet, it is somewhat slow compared to the others, in spite of its great power. It has, for instance, been banned from modern boxing along with the backfist, without anyone feeling that much has been lost by doing so. On the ground it is a different story. It is excellent there, as it does not rely so much on the twisting of the body or the moving of the legs to generate force, but rather on the up-and-down alignment of muscles

Hammer Fist Through Guard

through your torso and arm. This can make it much easier to deliver in many situations on the ground than the jab or cross.

Hammer Fist from Side Mount

But you still need to try to rotate your shoulder and hip into each strike as much as possible, as the twisting helps make your hammer fist land harder. As with all the fist strikes, strong hands are a must.

Elbow. From a standing position, the front of the elbow can be delivered in one of three ways: straight across horizontally at the face or side of the face, down to up going between your opponent's guarding hands and landing on the chin, or up to down. A fourth strike, a jab, is executed with the back of the elbow. Elbowing horizontally across the forehead can cut your antagonist, leading to a possible referee stoppage.

Elbow in the Clinch

The footwork and body rotation for the first three resemble those of the hook punch and for the fourth that of the jab punch. The elbow can be done with either the lead arm or back arm depending on the circumstances. It is great to combine elbowing with a single overhook grab. It can be done with or without a grip equally well and is a very powerful move. On the ground it is excellent to complement pins and to attack the turtle (more on turtling later).

The delivery area is the part of the forearm closest to the elbow. The target is the head. It is very grappling

Elbow from Side Mount

friendly. Flying elbows can come in handy.

Knee. The most powerful weapon in your arsenal is the knee. Its force has been compared to that of a truck.

While standing up, trap your opponent with the double overhook, bend his head down with your grip, pulling him around the floor off balance, and knee him repeatedly in the face.

You can also knee to the ribs, stomach, and legs. If you surprise your opponent at an opportune time, you can deliver a flying knee to

Flying Knee

Knee in the Clinch

the head, which is a stunningly spectacular, acrobatic move that drives the most force you can generate into your opponent's greatest area of vulnerability. Often a one- or two-step lead-up is required to generate the kind of height needed. When an opponent is tired and reacting slowly later in a match, this move can be very effective. Make sure you point your toes down as far as you can, as this makes your knee strike swifter. On the ground you can knee your adversary from almost every top position. This is quite

Knee in Side Mount

convenient because while your arms are busy keeping your opponent down, your knees can be charged with the task of bashing him into submission or worse. Targets for your knees on the ground are the ribs and head (if allowed by the rules).

Roundhouse Kick. While the knee certainly is powerful, it lacks the range of a kick. The roundhouse kick is the strongest kick. It is done either horizontally or

Roundhouse Kick to the Thigh

Roundhouse Kick to the Head

on an angle of 45 degrees or greater at any part of your adversary's body.

The angled version of this kick is often called the triangle kick, and it is quicker to deliver than the horizontal roundhouse.

When delivering any kick, bring the foot directly from the ground to the target along its prescribed course. Since MMA is a one-on-one sporting competition where your opponent is expecting your attack at all moments, if you bring your knee up first you will often telegraph what you are about to do. You do not want to do that. Doing the unexpected is at the heart of fighting strategy. The most common targets are your opponent's legs at the knee or thigh level on the inside or outside. But do not miss the chance to kick your adversary in the head or face if you are able to do so safely, particularly when he is getting tired and you are still feeling energetic. Roundhouse kicks at the torso region can work, but they can also be quite risky because the torso is well protected by the arms and sharp elbows, which can disturb your leg's motion and unbalance you or worse. All the same, scoring a good solid roundhouse kick to the ribs is a good thing to do whenever you can!

The best part of your leg to deliver the kick with is your shin rather than the top of your foot because of the chance of the little bones of your foot breaking if you hit with the foot. But your shin could also break, making toughening the shin very important for developing this technique into a useful tool for you. Shins are known to snap right in half when a kick is blocked with a stronger shin, leaving a horrible injury. You also need to be able to tolerate the pain and force of a shin-on-shin collision due to a block or a simultaneous attack. Hit the heavy bag and hard focus pads a lot. Be careful how you train and use this technique. Never do this move or anything else in this book except under the watchful eye of a qualified and experienced coach, and under the direction of a qualified physician.

It is more powerful to launch this kick with your rear leg than with your front, so that it can develop more momentum in its journey, like the cross punch using the rear arm. However, the kick still works if you strike with the front leg. Whichever leg you kick with, you need to rotate the foot that stays on the ground in the direction of the kick so that you can twist your whole body into the blow. Therefore, if your kick is going counterclockwise, your supporting foot should rotate counter-clockwise as well. If your kick is going clockwise, then your supporting foot is rotating clockwise also. Exactly how or when you rotate your planted foot will depend on the exigencies of the moment. You may find it better either to pivot on the ball of your supporting foot or to twist your foot in the air and set it on the ground simultaneously with or a moment before your kick's delivery. The roundhouse kick is a great move and can do a lot to take the fight out of your opponent.

Because the legs support the whole body, softening up your adversary's legs through repeated kicks to them can do a lot to help you win a match. One good basic drill is to practice alternately kicking with a back leg roundhouse and a front leg jab kick, as this combination is as important for the feet as the jab–power punch combination is for the hands. If you watch yourself do this in the mirror, it looks really impressive, like you are a kung fu expert or something—great for the ego and your overall confidence level! On the ground, if your opponent is loosely in your guard, you might be able to kick into the side of his head with your heel, or even straight into his face.

Push Kick. Also known as the jab kick, the push kick is a really great kick. It is to the legs what the jab punch is to the arms. While it is not as devastating as the roundhouse kick, it is still very strong. Tactically it is extremely important. An advancing adversary can be push kicked in the stomach under his arms, and he will be stopped immediately. An opponent can be pushed back with the kick when too close for comfort. The push kick is normally unleashed on the stomach area and the upper legs. Your opponent's kicks can be stopped by counter kicking the thigh of the attacking leg. While you are on the ground, your adversary's attempts to put leg locks on you can often be thwarted by pushing him off your leg with a jab kick from your free leg. You can even use this kick as a kind of heel kick to the face when the adversary is in your guard on the ground and is not being careful. In this case it can be delivered directly or with some circularity.

The push kick is done by raising your front leg directly up and driving the ball of your foot or your heel into your opponent's stomach or thighs. Do not bring your knee up first and then send your foot out in two motions unless the specific situation dictates that you do so.

Raising your knee first before thrusting out your foot slows your action down and allows your supporting leg to be chopped out with a swift counter kick. Rotate your hip forward to get more power and more distance as you jab your foot out. You will be quite surprised by how much reach you can get with this kick.

Even if you watch someone else perform it, you will be amazed at how far its effective range is. After it is done, set your foot right back down in front of you.

If you throw a push kick with the rear leg, the same rules apply. Twist your hip forward and stab your foot directly out into your opponent. You can then set the rear foot in front to change the side that is forward in your fighting stance from left to right or from right to left. Using the back foot gives you more reach than using the front foot, so the back foot push kick can be used to cover more distance in your attack. It is slower, however, and therefore easier for your adversary to notice and take evasive action against. It is therefore not used as much as the front leg jab kick. When delivering a kick with the back leg, the roundhouse is almost always to be preferred.

For all kicks, leg strength is very important, as are balance, accuracy, flexibility, toughness, and especially speed. You need to make your legs strong and fast. Do lots of skipping and run-

Push Kick: Starting High   **Push Kick: End**

ning, and of course huge numbers of repetitions against the heavy bag and focus mitts for power and accuracy. The legs are about four times stronger than the arms, and they can deliver heavier strikes. It is well worth your time mastering the art of kicking. Mix kicks in with punches as part of your solo training, and get skillful at delivering killer combinations. Keep in mind that of the four main strikes, the jab and cross punches and the jab and roundhouse kicks, it is the cross punch and the roundhouse kick delivered with your rear leg that are the stronger ones.

One special weakness of the push kick in MMA is that the kicking leg is liable to be caught in the hands or hooked with the crook of the elbow of the opponent, leading to a single leg throw. Be aware of this when concocting strategies for the ring. The roundhouse kick is harder to catch.

Another benefit of the push kick is that it can be done from the knee up shielding position. After guarding yourself against kicks with the knee up, you can thrust your foot out at your opponent in retaliation. Sometimes you will do this merely to get space by pushing your opponent away or pushing off from him to launch yourself backward.

Side Kick. From the knee up shielding position, you can deliver a side kick with the heel by rotating your foot so its inner edge is facing the ground and thrusting your heel into your opponent, usually into the ribs.

Because launching a side kick changes the angle of attack somewhat from what is expected by a basic push kick from this position, you might be able to score a solid and undefended hit with it.

Spinning Back Kick. This kick is done to catch your opponent off guard. Because it is powerful and disorienting to your opponent, the spinning back kick is a worthwhile technique to attempt when the situation calls for it. Because it involves turning your back for an instant, however, the spinning back kick

Side Kick

Spinning Back Kick

has its risks and must be used with discretion. Assuming your right foot is in front, pivot on it counterclockwise while bringing up your left knee. As your body is rotating around on the right foot, extend the heel of your left foot out and into your opponent's ribs or other worthwhile target.

Your final position will look very much like that of a completed side kick. Your method of getting to that position, however, is quite different from that of the side kick.

DEFENSES AGAINST STRIKES

You are in the ring to defeat your opponent, but since this can take some time to accomplish, you need to also make sure that your adversary does not beat you while you are at it. This is why defense is important, although not as important as attack. To explain this, think of two fighters, one only attacking and the other only defending. Eventually the attacker will score hits and the defender will lose. Also, by attacking, you make your opponent defend, preventing him or her from attacking you. Therefore, attacking has a defensive value that sometimes gets overlooked. In this sense, you need to think of defense as a means to prevent attack and also to retaliate. It is for this reason that the arms are normally kept cocked by your face, as they are a shield, but also ready at all times to lash out at your opponent. Your legs are kept in a ready position to attack at all times as well; supporting you while you stand is a secondary function as their primary purpose in MMA is to unleash havoc on your adversary. The arms can parry blows by moving very slightly from their shielding positions: up and down, left and right. The forearms can change their angles to deal with various attacks.

This means that you do not have to waste much energy and time on defense. Instead you can focus on beating your opponent, both literally and figuratively.

Old boxing manuals from the nineteenth century, when the sport was often done bare-knuckled, have all the same kinds of blocks and parries we find in karate, kung fu, and other

Defending Strikes
Adam (left) defends strikes from Chris.

martial arts today. The first modern boxing trainers in seventeenth-century England based their methods on fencing, which makes a lot of sense. The forearms take the place of the sword blade, and they can do all the same kinds of parries, thrusts, and chops that a sword can do. Parrying an outside punch to the inside makes for a good example. Knocking your adversary's right hand punch to your right with the inside of your left forearm is highly recommended whenever you are forced to parry because you put your opponent in a position where his arms are both turned away from you but where both of yours are available to strike him. If you can combine parrying a kick with grappling the foot up for a throw, that is great too. You first absorb the kick with your shin, shoulder, or forearm, and once the impetus of the kick is spent, you immediately grip under the leg with whatever arm is available and take your opponent down.

In MMA you can wrestle with your opponent, so parries can often turn into grips such as the single overhook, double overhook, and double underhook as your arm or arms collide with your opponent's and then snake around his body to control it. With this in mind you can see how grip fighting and parrying are linked skills, and in the same breath you can see how stopping a grappling attack is every bit as important as stopping a striking one.

The best way to block a leg attack is by parrying it with your own leg. Just bring your knee up and form a shield with your shin perpendicular to the ground. To form a nearly full body shield, raise your shin on one side of your body and place that side's elbow outside the knee, keeping your other arm cocked in the on guard position. If you put your elbow on the inside, the shield is weaker against powerful strikes. It is even possible to start punches and kicks from this position in the midst of an opponent's attack.

Shin Blocking Opposite-Side Kick

Just as in warfare on the battlefield, the best defense is distance. And just as soldiers remain out of each other's rifle range and then sneak or rush in to attack each other without warning, so you must learn to use distancing in your attacks and defenses. Your jab kick will serve you well to create distance, either through simply stopping your adversary in his tracks, pushing him back, or launching yourself back. The jab punch can serve the same purpose closer up. Moving yourself a bit to the side but a little forward too can take you out of the direct line of your opponent's attack and enable you to score hits. Even jumping up can move your body out of the position your opponent expects it to be in and allows you to deliver a sudden flying technique like a flying knee or superman punch. The one caution is against lowering yourself down to change the angle of your attack or defense. This can make you vulnerable to knees and other blows to the face, although if you score a takedown and get top position on the ground, it was well worth it. A cowardly strategy, however, is no good. You have to be on the attack, wanting generally to advance on your adversary, being happy to get in for a clinch and deliver knees and perform throws. You should want to go to the ground taking top position there. The best defense is a relentless offense.

BASIC GROUND SKILLS:
WRESTLING, PINS, ESCAPES, AND SUBMISSIONS

The wrestling and grappling moves to follow are as difficult to learn and master as the striking moves in the previous chapter. They require a different form of study as well, because to become proficient at executing them you must have a partner at all times. At first you will need a passive partner who simply allows you to get in and out of position a number of times. After you understand how to do the move and are fairly quick at applying it, have your partner resist a little, and then gradually add more and more resistance until what you are doing is essentially a full-out attack and defense, like a little five-second or so piece of a real MMA match. Always, of course, put safety first, because if you or your helpers are injured, you cannot train. Safety is of paramount concern. Do not make your movements too swift or too powerful right off the bat, and of course, do not hit your training partners too hard.

Because grappling and wrestling involve gripping, developing a strong grip is essential for being able to make the techniques work. Exercises that develop a strong grip are crucial for MMA. Weights, rope climbing, grappling with a partner, and so on, are all ways to improve grip strength.

Throws and Defenses

The dominant grip for throwing is the double underhook. This grip is formed by placing the crooks of both your elbows under your opponent's armpits and applying a lifting force to his or her body. This raises his or her center of balance and makes achieving a throw relatively easy. However, most throws can be done from an over-under grip too. If caught in a double underhook, it is sometimes possible to pull off a whizzer, meaning a spinning throw trapping your opponent's arms under your armpits, but it is quite risky. Specialized throws like the shoulder throw work from grips that on their own are not very strong and therefore rely on speed and surprise for their effectiveness. Whenever you are in a grip fight, be sure to consider striking where reasonably possible. If you have good reach and like striking, remember that all your wonderful striking abilities are completely nullified if you can be taken down to the floor. Striking, clinch work, and throwing all have to go hand in hand.

In MMA your ability to fight in the clinch is crucial. It is the pivot point of the match. If you are afraid of the clinch, you will always be running away from your opponent. If you are good at the clinch, you can win with knees and establish a dominant position on the ground with a good throw. The clinch is a terrifically volatile part of the fight. Not only is each competitor's body subject to violent knee and other strikes from up close, but his balance is at stake as well. In the blink of an eye, one or the other fighter could go crashing to the ground with the other on top.

The part of the fight in the clinch is not the longest due to how volatile it is: someone will get hit hard, get thrown, or slip up and fall, or the two competitors might disengage. While a fighter can end a clinch with a good strike like a knee to the head, the clinch tends to either lead to the ground or back to the free standing stage. If it goes to the ground, the person on top has a big advantage but it still might take a long time to completely finish the downed opponent. If the two clinchers disengage from one another standing, the fatigue of the clinch fighting will bear down more heavily on the less prepared one, leading to an advantage for his opponent in striking, etcetera.

The position you are working for in the clinch is either the double overhook (both hands placed behind your opponent's head, pulling his head down) to use the knee or the double underhook to throw your adversary. If you have taken a double overhook grip but are countered with a double underhook, you have to quickly swim your arms under to get a double underhook grip to prevent your opponent from throwing you. You also need to establish this grip if your opponent is keeping his head too high and you cannot bend it down to feed it into your knee.

Often your opponent will respond to your double underhook by snaking his arms back under yours to take his own double underhook grip again. This activity to get the dominant grip is called pummeling and is done on its own as a form of grip training. Throwing in strikes like the elbow to the face from a single overhook, or suddenly removing a shoulder in order to swing in for a punch, or getting knees into the torso and head, are all things to consider to help you get that dominant grip. One caution though is that if you are too focused on the achievement of the double underhook, your opponent could quickly grapple up your legs for a double leg throw or some other trick.

Do not forget about the whizzer grip. All of the spinning throws mentioned in this section can be done as whizzers. Still, the whizzer is a very risky move against a skilled wrestler as it involves giving up the dominant underhook grip to your opponent and hoping that while spinning you will actually throw him and not simply end up being pushed onto your face with your opponent over your back. Spending lots of time actually wrestling with partners is a necessity for becoming proficient at mixed martial arts.

DOUBLE LEG THROW

This is a good throw to drill both in the capacity of attacker and as defender. It is one of the very best throws in mixed martial arts because fighters' thoughts are often occupied with upright striking concerns, and they can sometimes forget about the possibility of having their legs taken out from under them. The actual delivery of this move is simple: hug both of your opponent's legs at the knees where they buckle in together and tackle him to the ground.

You might end up in your adversary's guard, or you might be able to skirt around it during the takedown. Just watch that you do not get kneed in the head as you lower yourself.

Sprawling is the major defense to the double leg throw. For this reason, some fighters' combat style is referred to as

Double Leg Throw

sprawling and brawling, as they prefer to keep the fight standing and do so primarily by avoiding takedowns with the double leg throw. If you cannot avoid being thrown with this technique, then all your striking skills are for naught. On the offense, it is one of several good methods of taking down your opponent and ending up on top as a response to his double leg throw attempt.

Sprawling
Chris (right) is sprawling to avoid a double leg throw.

SINGLE LEG THROW

In this throw, you hook one of your opponent's legs with one of your arms and push him down backward. It is useful when your opponent has raised a leg off the floor for any reason, either for a kick or to block one of your kicks, for example. There are many ways to do the single leg depending on the circumstances. You can trap the leg with an over grip or an under grip.

You might grip closer to the ankle or to the knee. Your other arm might have an underhook grip or might not. You might hold the leg with both your arms or with only one. You might even hack out your opponent's other, supporting, leg with one of your own.

The only way to learn to apply the single leg is to do live wrestling where both of you are actively trying for it, and to

Single Leg Throw from Inside of Thigh

Single Leg Throw from Outside of Thigh

make use of it in mixed sparring bouts. Real opponents do not just stand there and let you throw them down!

BACK THROW

This is another excellent technique. To perform it, you need your legs behind your adversary so that you are both facing in more or less the same direction, but your opponent is in front of you. Use either a bear hug grip (holding your opponent tightly around the belly from behind) or another similar one and rotate your opponent down over the top of one of your legs.

Back Throw
Chris (on left) performs a back throw on Adam.

Back Throw Follow-Up on Ground
Mickey (the thrower) on the left prepares to mount Adam.

You should land on the ground with your legs in position to be quickly wrapped around your adversary so that you can establish a full or back mount.

SWEEPING HIP THROW

From a double underhook or even over-under grip, you turn in to throw your opponent over your hip, but to make matters worse for him, you sweep your leg on that side back and take his supporting leg on that side out of the picture while casting your opponent over and down in a large impressive and crashing movement. The use of your leg to sweep helps to prevent your adversary from stepping around and out of your grip.

INNER THIGH THROW

This throw can be done, like many of the throws, standing or on the ground. It is very much like the sweeping hip throw, but your sweeping leg is brought between your opponent's legs and takes out the inner leg at the thigh rather than the outer leg. The inner thigh throw happens to be one of the most common throws in judo competitions, and it is also very useful in no *gi* situations such as MMA fights or wrestling matches.

It can even be done as a defense to your opponent pressing your turtle down, if you can grapple one of his arms in tight under one of your shoulders and twist through with it.

SHOULDER THROW

This is a surprise technique. Since it involves turning your back from a nondominant grip, it must be looked at as risky, but it can be good for situations where you are being dominated in the grip fighting, or where your turtle is being pressed down upon on the ground.

Gripping your adversary's wrist with one hand, you trap his armpit between the biceps and forearm of your other arm and turn in to throw. Placing your foot on that side outside of his same-side foot is advisable to stop him from escaping. You

Sweeping Hip Throw

Inner Thigh Throw

Shoulder Throw

can also perform this throw by falling to your knees, using the sudden change in weight distribution to unbalance your opponent over your shoulders.

WINDING THROW

The winding throw operates precisely like the shoulder throw except instead of trapping your opponent's armpit with your biceps and forearm, you trap his upper arm tightly with your armpit and roll. It is especially important in this throw to keep your same-side foot to the outside of your opponent's. The winding throw is a particularly good technique to use to escape a situation where you are turtling and your opponent is wrapping his arms around your chest or belly. If you can trap his arm on one side, you can easily perform the throw on the ground.

HOOK THROWS

There are a variety of these. From a strong grip, hook one of your opponent's legs with one of yours and throw your adversary over your hooking leg.

You can hook either of your opponent's legs with either of yours, attacking it from either the outside or the inside. There are therefore eight permutations of this throw. The best one to pull off is a same-side-to-same-side (right-leg-to-right-leg or left-leg-to-left-leg) outer hook throw, since you will land on the ground outside your adversary's guard. All the other varieties land

Winding Throw from Turtle
As Chris (white trunks) is about to take Mickey's back, Mickey throws him.

Outer Hook Throw
Mickey (in black) performs an outer hook throw.

Inner Hook Throw

Wrapping Hook Throw

you inside your opponent's full or half guard, albeit on top of him there.

Any hook throw can be easily reversed if you do not unbalance your adversary well in its execution.

FOOT SWEEPS

These are very important for keeping your opponent off balance. They are the jabs of the wrestling world. While lifting up with a good grip and rotating the opposite way from your sweep, you sweep one of your opponent's feet at the side or back of the heel area with the sole of one of your own.

As with the hook throws, there are eight versions of this technique. Foot sweeps must be done very quickly to work. Be ready to follow up with a throw in the opposite direction if your foot sweep fails to take your opponent down.

Foot Sweep

PUSH DOWN THROW

If your opponent is bending forward and you can pull him right down onto the floor, then go right ahead! Sometimes you will be able to do this when your opponent is fatigued or when he stumbles or makes an ineffective double or single leg throw attempt.

This is a common follow-up, for instance, after you have sprawled. It can be done either from a double overhook grip or simply by pushing down on the back of a stumbling or lunging forward opponent, while you jump your legs back out of the range of his arms. Immediately upon pushing your opponent down, keep the pressure down on his back while spinning your legs around behind him.

Now you can consider what kind of turtle attacks you want to launch. The knee strike is done from a very similar starting

Push Down Throw: Start
Mickey thwarts Chris's double leg attempt by pushing him down.

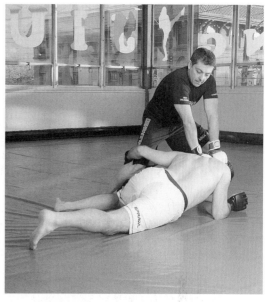

Push Down Throw: Finish

position to this one, and you might combine the two techniques together or not depending on your strategy at the time.

This throw is also done when your opponent's attempt to turn in for a spinning throw fails. You will be able to push him down to the ground and follow up there, staying on his back.

Pins and Escapes

In MMA it is a simple rule that the person on top is in the dominant position. This is due to the law of gravity identified by Sir Isaac Newton. Gravity is a very strong force on us, and it regulates everything we do in life. It also governs everything we do in the arena. Fighting gravity is hard enough. Fighting gravity and another person on top of you as well is extremely hard. For this reason you must strive to achieve top position on the ground and maintain it. The only time you will sacrifice a top for bottom position is when you are certain of your ability to wind in for a final submission move. Normally, your goal from the top position is to deliver strikes such as knees, elbows, punches, and hammer fists, primarily to your opponent's head, but also to his ribs. The skill is in keeping your adversary pinned down and in place while you generate windup space for your hits.

Generally, the way out of a pin involves you spinning your entire body clockwise or counterclockwise as the situation dictates, choosing the path of least resistance. To be able to spin, you need to first generate enough space to do so. There are often a number of ways to do this including pushing off, jolting, and even waiting for your opponent to release the pressure a little while he transitions into another move or winds up to strike. You will find your elbows, knees and hips, and even head to be important posting points to generate push off, space, and rotating power. Arching the back and randomly thrusting the hips upward are also very important. Getting hands, knees, and elbows in between you and your opponent is also part of escaping. Once this is achieved, "shrimping" can be employed, which is shooting the hips out backward away from your opponent, making you look like a swimming shrimp. Specific escapes are covered in the following sections for each pin.

GUARD

The guard is the name given to the position by Brazilian Jiu-Jitsu experts, who have been very active in the development of its use. The position is one where the bottom player, on his back, has wrapped his legs around the opponent's trunk, waist, or outer thighs.

A skillful grappler has little to fear from an untutored brawler in his guard as there are numerous ways to flip the attacker over, called sweeps, and to achieve effective submissions through chokes and joint locks.

The triangle choke is particularly effective for attacking someone in your guard. The term *guard* comes from the fact that you can defend yourself quite well on the ground with it against an unskilled or less skilled grappler. *Closed guard* refers to when you hook your feet together over your adversary's back, squeezing in with your thighs. *Open guard* describes the guard position when you do not have your feet attached together like this.

Guard (Front View)

However, as discussed previously, when fighting another skilled grappler, gravity provides the person on top with an advantage. The person on top can strike the one on the bottom, pass his guard, or disengage and force the fight back up to the standing position.

Guard (Side View)

From the bottom, a fighter will have a hard time catching another skilled grappler with the triangle choke or a sweep, and an even harder time with a guillotine. The bottom fighter cannot disengage at will, cannot strike very effectively, and is facing fatigue trying to defend against the passing and striking attempts of the person on top. This is why in MMA, as well as in Brazilian Jiu-Jitsu tournaments, the top position is sought.

You absolutely must know how to handle the guard if you want to be a mixed martial arts fighter. Even if you can dominate the clinch and throw your adversary into a guard situation, if you are not skillful enough to do anything but crouch on top of him from that point on, you will be a rather one-dimensional fighter. It can be quite draining to fight through the guard, but it is even more draining for the person on the bottom trying to keep you from doing so. If the clinch is the most volatile position in MMA, the guard is certainly the second most important.

Backing Out of a Guard
Chris (in white) backs out from Mickey's guard.

First of all, in a mixed martial arts competition, you can strike, so make sure you do so. While in your opponent's guard, get yourself into what you could call a horse or straddle stance, well balanced and stable, similar to what you see in karate and kung fu training. Keep your knees flexed and your upper body relatively upright. This will seem very difficult to do at first. You have to train against a fighting opponent to be able to establish and keep this position while in someone's guard in a real match. But it is the best position from which to attack the guard. From this very stable straddle stance, use the windup in your legs and torso you now have to punch your adversary's face. You will have to bend down into your strikes to make them land. It takes training to get good at this, but that simply means that you must train hard for it. You might be able to score a knock-out or referee stoppage if you are good at this. The whole time you have to be able to ensure your opponent does not pull off a sweep against you and topple you over onto the ground. You need to train to stand up in the guard like this while grappling against a training partner who is trying his best to sweep you down or submit you.

Since it is much easier to strike your opponent's face when you are closer to it, keep looking to pass your adversary's guard to establish the full mount position (more on the full mount later). Your continuous barrage of strikes helps take your opponent's mind off your passing attempts. If you have not been able to get up into a straddle stance and are fighting from your knees, you can still strike at your opponent's face with punches and hammer fists, and you can still pass of course, but everything will be harder and take longer to do. At the least, keep your knees well apart to establish a firm base. You might find yourself staying on your knees from fatigue or loss of sense of balance. This is why training to endure the rigors of MMA fighting is key in your preparation. If you are on your knees and unable to stand up into the straddle stance, you might consider disengaging by stepping up and back from your opponent's guard, keeping one or both of his knees controlled with one or both of your hands.

KNEE THROUGH PASS

This pass is the easiest to achieve. While you are punching your downed opponent in his guard, forcefully slide one of your knees over and across your adversary's inner thigh. You can slide either knee over either thigh.

If you are passing with your right knee, you can slide it over the opponent's right or left inner thigh and plant your knee and entire lower leg on the ground on the side of his body you have gotten it to.

If you are able to, you can keep pressing the thigh down with your ankle and foot to keep your opponent's legs wide apart so you can easily slide your other knee through as well.

One way or another, bring your trailing leg through as well and plant it on the ground too. If you bring your right knee across

Knee Through Pass: Start
Mickey deftly slides his knee over Chris's left thigh.

Knee Through Pass: End
Mickey has now gotten his leg through, advancing to Chris's half guard.

Knee Through Pass: Keeping the Legs Opened
Mickey keeps Adam's legs opened by leaving his foot over Adam's left inner thigh and pressing down.

Knee Through Pass: Finish in Full Mount
Mickey can get his left knee through because Adam's legs were kept opened. Mickey can now establish full mount, which is better than getting stuck in half guard.

your opponent's right thigh, when you finish bringing your left leg through as well, you will be holding your opponent in the side mount. If you bring your right knee across your adversary's left thigh, you will be able to establish a full mount.

Full mount is better than side mount, but it is easier for your opponent to ensnare your left leg between his while you are passing if you employ this right knee across left thigh technique. This can result in a half-guard situation, which is better for the fighter on top than remaining in full guard, but it is not yet a full pass. Therefore, which side to pass on depends more on the feeling of the moment, following the path of least resistance, as each side has its positives and negatives.

HOP OVER PASS
This pass is a kind of extreme version of the knee through pass. While keeping your adversary busy worrying about the punches

Hop Over Pass: Start

Hop Over Pass: End with Punch

you are punishing his face with, you hop through and over the inner thighs and directly into a full mount.

Obviously this is not a technique to employ when your opponent is gripping you tightly with his legs but is rather one to use when there is a fair bit of space and your opponent is distracted or tired.

Besides leaping directly over and landing in full mount, you can leap circularly over either of your opponent's legs, clockwise or counterclockwise, spinning over through the air into a side mount position. You might want to place one or both of your hands on your adversary's belly as a pivot point.

SCOOP PASS

This is a very reliable pass. Hook your arm under your opponent's calf or heel on the same side, squeezing it between your biceps and forearm, and rotate that leg up and forward.

While up, press and slide your head into and around your adversary's ankle area, getting your head to the outside of his leg, keeping the pressure on, and pushing your opponent's leg over and across toward his other leg.

You should be able now to simply pounce into a side mount position on your opponent. Conversely, if you feel you cannot just pounce forward like this, you can press your adversary's hooked leg down to the ground by pushing down on it with your underarm and then rolling forward along your shoulder blades and up his body, spinning over into a side mount. So, if you're pinning down your opponent's left leg under your right armpit, you would roll clockwise along your shoulder blades up his hip and belly and spin into a side mount on his left side.

The obvious worry in all this is that if you end up hooking your arm under your opponent's leg at his thigh instead of at the calf or ankle, you could find your adversary pulling you into a triangle choke. However, this is what training is for. You need to

Scoop Pass Kneeling: Start
Mickey scoops Chris's leg with his right elbow crook.

Scoop Pass with Head Past

Scoop Pass Standing: Start
Mickey scoops Chris's leg at the calf with his right elbow crook.

do lots of grappling as part of your training, and passing guard and avoiding getting submitted in the process is part and parcel of it. In the ring, may the best man win!

SCISSORS SWEEP

Sweeps can be difficult to pull off in no *gi* MMA matches. Still, they can be done, and often they are the best hope of the bottom fighter. Sweeps refer to taking down someone in your guard and ending up on top of him. The double underhook grip is preferable for the sweeps, but at the moment of an opponent's imbalance quite a variety of grips besides this one can also be effective.

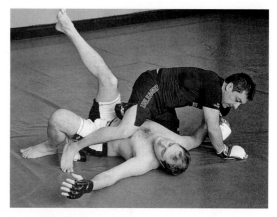

Scissors Sweep: Start
Mickey (in black) is sweeping Chris (in white).

Scissors Sweep: End

To execute a scissors sweep, hug your opponent in tight to your chest while blocking one of his thighs with one of yours.

Let us say you are blocking your opponent's right thigh with your left. If your opponent is not a good grappler, you might be able to flip him over with only this. However, you usually have to add another element to it. Bring your right knee up to your chest and place your shin along your opponent's left rib cage, hooking the top of your foot around his or her flank. Make sure your adversary's right arm is not posting on the ground.

Now, roll him over to your left so your adversary is on his back and you can establish full mount.

ELEVATOR SWEEP

The elevator sweep works in essentially the same way as the scissors sweep, but you hook the top of your right foot under your adversary's groin or thigh and "elevate" him with your right foot while blocking his right thigh with your left thigh and rotating both of your bodies together, all in one motion.

Elevator Sweep, Part 1
Adam thrusts his leg under Chris's groin area.

Elevator Sweep, Part 2
Chris is sent flying.

BUTTERFLY GUARD AND BUTTERFLY ELEVATOR SWEEP

The butterfly guard is like getting in position to do elevator sweeps with both feet at once.

Insert both of your feet under your opponent's groin or thighs, allowing your knees to splay outward to prevent him from passing around them on either side.

You need to use your feet very much like hooks and continually threaten to lift your opponent right off the ground with them, like a butterfly in flight.

Butterfly Guard (Front View)

Butterfly Guard (Side View)

Butterfly Elevator Sweep: Start

If you squeeze your opponent in tight with your arms, you can easily launch him or her right over your head and land on top in full mount. This is called a butterfly elevator sweep.

Butterfly Elevator Sweep: Midway
Chris (in white) is now unbalanced and is being rolled over.

The butterfly guard is a better guard option than the basic guard because it has much more offensive potential. It is definitely a technique to master.

HALF GUARD

In a half guard you trap one of your opponent's legs between both of yours while you are on your back. It is only half as good a defense as the basic guard, since your opponent has a fair amount of stability to use against you for striking. However, just as with the other guards, if you are able to pull your opponent's upper body in tightly to you, or shift your hips quickly, you might be able to get your inside foot underneath his groin or thigh and pull off an elevator sweep. Conversely, you might be able, if you have, say, his right leg trapped between yours, to pull his torso in close, turn your hips clockwise so you are on your right hip, and establish a kind of side hold on your adversary. From here you can shift your weight on top of his back while keeping the leg grappled up between yours and actually establish a face down pin called a leg ride!

If you are in your opponent's half guard, focus on punching him or her in the face with knuckle punches and hammer fists.

Good training to keep yourself from getting swept from this position is important. If you want to, you can pass the half guard by bringing your knee through and over your opponent's groin or inner thigh. If you bring it through on the side your other leg is on, it is a bit easier than pressing it over the other side. But if you slide it through into full mount, you end up in a better finishing position. In MMA, the half guard is a rather dominant position for the one on top because of the striking possibilities from it.

Half Guard
Chris (in white) is in Mickey's half guard.

Punching Opponent While in His Half Guard

GETTING BACK TO YOUR FEET FROM GUARD

Being on your back in mixed martial arts is a bad thing. You do not want to stay there long. Ideally you want to get up without exposing your back to your opponent. So practice, from a guard position, bringing one foot back underneath your hips and standing up on it while swinging your other leg back and into position.

Getting Back to Your Feet from Guard, Part 1
Mickey puts his foot under his hips.

Getting Back to Your Feet from Guard, Part 2
Mickey gets his other foot back and gets up to a crouch.

You naturally have to use your hands too at first, as if doing a crab walk. This is something that takes some getting used to through repetitive training. If your opponent is in your guard, you first have to push off with your foot into his thigh on one side, scoot your hips back, and then immediately place that foot under your hips and finish the movement as detailed above.

Getting Back to Your Feet from Guard, Part 3
Mickey stands up ready to fight.

TURTLE

If your opponent is on all fours, this is called turtling. In MMA, you do not need to flip your adversary onto his back from this position as you would in wrestling or often would in judo. Because striking is a part of mixed martial arts, you can consider yourself now in a dominant position. Keep your opponent from standing up by pressing your chest or forearms down on his back, or in some other way. Then hit your opponent's head with hammer fists, elbows, and knees.

In most wrestling styles around the world, turtling loses the match, which reflects how bad a position this is on the battlefield or in any kind of real fighting, including MMA. However, the turtler might be able to achieve a leg throw if the opponent's legs are within reach.

Holding Down and Punching the Turtle

If you cannot finish the fight with strikes, you can apply a rear naked choke by straddling your opponent's back at the waist and hooking your heels into his or her groin area. You can deliver some softening-up blows to your adversary's head from this position and/or immediately apply the choke hold. To finish the choke you have to thrust forward with your hips while pulling back with your heels and your arms. This will flatten him out onto the floor. This choke is detailed under its own heading.

LEG RIDE

Another strategy for handling the turtle is to use the leg ride. Trap one of your adversary's thighs between both of yours while gripping his upper body tightly and keeping your body weight pressing down on his back. Pull back with your legs and press forward with your hips so that the trapped leg is tightly ensnared. From this position it is possible to flatten your opponent right out.

Leg Throw from Turtle
The turtler (Chris, in white) retaliates with a double leg throw.

Leg Ride
Chris has grappled up Adam's leg from behind.

FACE DOWN

An opponent might use a face down position, flat out on the floor, to momentarily stop you from getting one or both of your heels in while attempting a rear naked choke.

You need to be quick enough to realize that you can now throw some strikes at his head without much fear of being rolled over.

If you have flattened your adversary out like this on purpose by pressing down on his back, you can apply myriad strikes to his head. It is not a bad idea to straddle your opponent's waist, and when he tries to get back up onto his hands and knees, to get your hooks (heels) into your adversary's groin and fight for the rear naked choke.

Face Down
Mickey is punching Adam, who is in the face down position, in the head.

BACK CONTROL

To achieve back control, you need to first get to your opponent's back. You can do this by forcing your adversary down to a turtle position from standing with a push down or by getting to a leg ride position. If you are lucky, your opponent will mistakenly open the door for you by simply giving you his back while turning or spinning. However you may get there, and regardless of whether you are on top or on the bottom, get your legs around your opponent's waist and hook your heels into his groin or inner thigh area. Press forward strongly with your hips while pulling back forcefully with your heels. Get your arms around his throat and ideally slide one of them under his chin, pulling back strongly with your arms too.

You should be able to make your opponent's back arch, rendering him totally helpless. The objective here is the rear naked choke.

Back Control Face Down

Back Control Face Up

FULL MOUNT

In this position you are straddling your opponent's waist or chest while he is lying on his back. You can punch your adversary's face while riding out his attempts to shake you off with sudden upward twisting hip thrusts and back arches.

To get an opponent off of you who is pinning you in full mount, you need to bring back, say, your left heel and trap your adversary's right ankle between your heel and your left hip. Then, knocking or otherwise ensuring his right hand is not posting on the ground to prevent it, roll counterclockwise. There will be nothing to stop you from rolling your adversary over. You will end up in his guard, but that is a good thing. You are now on top.

Full Mount

SIDE MOUNT

This is also known as side control. You are pinning your opponent down from the side. Your knees can either press up against his flank, or you can extend your legs almost straight out behind you, keeping yourself up on your toes. There are a few different positions for your arms. Your forearms might be pressing down on your adversary's chest, your elbows might be right over pressing against his flank or neck opposite your legs, and you might even have a forearm under your opponent's head or pressing down on his throat from above.

It is possible to deliver knees, elbows, and hammer fist strikes from the side mount. The best submission available from here is the americana armlock (discussed later). In terms of stability, the side mount is one of the most stable of all the pins because your downed opponent has nothing under your lower body to disturb your balance. The only problem with it is that while you are delivering strikes to your opponent's ribs and head with knees and arms, your opponent has some space to try to turn, get his knee on your thighs, push off, and escape. So this pin is normally used as a transitional pin to achieve full mount.

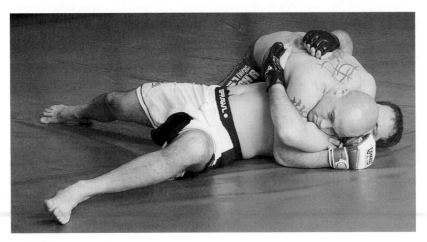

Side Mount

KNEE ON BELLY

This pin is also used transitionally. From some form of side control, let us say one where your knees are to your opponent's right side, you slide up and press your right knee down firmly into your adversary's belly, squishing it in and keeping him pinned down with it. Your left leg you brace straight out, with your foot posted into the ground so that it is out of reach of your opponent's arm.

From here you can hit your adversary's face with your fists and aim to slide your left knee right across in order to establish full mount.

SCARF HOLD

From some throws and from any position where you have an over-under grip on the ground, you can establish a very strong pin called the scarf hold. It has this name because your arm is like a scarf around your opponent's neck.

Knee on Belly

Scarf Hold

Let us assume that you have landed on the ground on top
of your adversary with your right arm over your opponent's left
shoulder and your legs out on his right side. Grip your right arm
tightly around and under his neck and squeeze, keeping your
elbow on the floor for stability. Press into your opponent's chest
with your chest. Trap your adversary's right arm under your left
armpit and circle your hand in under his right armpit, and tie
the knot tightly. Stretch your legs out straight, your right foot
far out from his head and your left foot far out from his lower
body. Your feet will be making contact with the floor with their
side edges. Press into your opponent's right rib cage with your
right rib cage while gripping tightly with your arms and keeping
your legs firm and stable. You should even press your forehead
into his right temple, keeping your opponent's head pushed into
the ground. This pressure, particularly in the ribs, will cause
some fatigue for your adversary because of the difficulty breathing, which is good for you. From this pin you can transition to
two submissions directly: the scarf lock and the hand triangle.

If you have not trained enough in grappling, or you are too
fatigued to apply a strong scarf hold, your opponent will be
able to trap up your nearest leg between his and start a leg ride,

or even just simply slide out, or at worst completely take your back. The scarf hold is the strongest pin there is, but making even a slight mistake can give your back to your opponent, so it is risky, albeit sometimes well worth the risk!

A strong variant grip is to hold your right thigh with your right hand, which you are controlling your adversary's neck with. Doing this allows your left arm to deliver strikes to your opponent's face.

A pin that is a kind of mix of the side mount and the scarf hold is one where you use the leg positions of the scarf hold, but you keep a rough double underhook grip on your adversary's shoulders, or an over-under hold. You can think of it as a scarf hold with a variant grip.

To get out of a scarf hold, get your elbow on the side of the hold down on the ground, and then get your knee on that side to more or less connect with your elbow. Shrimping your hips out helps with this. This position looks something like a lying down version of the kickboxing shielding position. Getting to it essentially breaks the effectiveness of the hold, as it generates the kind of space you need to either slip out or, more aggressively, actively take the back of your opponent or flip him over to the other side over your body by gripping tightly with your other arm too and rolling.

NORTH-SOUTH

In this pin, you are chest-to-chest, but aligned in opposite directions, with your legs out past your opponent's head.

Because being straight over your opponent is rare in a fight, this position tends to look and function like a side mount. However, it is different because your elbows can press into your adversary's armpits, and your knees can deliver blows to the top of your opponent's head. Beware though of your downed opponent kneeing *you* in the head from here!

To get out of a north-south pin, you need to fight to spin around over to your stomach.

North-South

BACKWARD HOLD

This is not a position you will tend to aim to get into, but it is important to know in case you have to use it. It is the reverse, more or less, of the scarf hold. Instead of facing toward your adversary's head, you are turned toward his feet. Assuming your legs are out toward his right side, you will have your left rib cage and armpit pressing down hard on your adversary's belly, and your left elbow on the ground pressed up against his left waist. Your right forearm will normally be applying downward pressure against your opponent's upper thighs, hip, or knees.

You are vulnerable here to some annoying hammer fists to the back of your head, so you should try to progress to a side mount by turning clockwise. It is also possible to roll counterclockwise over your shoulder blades to achieve a high side mount or north-south pin. You might try to add in an elbow to the face as part of the deal.

Backward Hold

Submissions and Getting Out of Them

To get any submission on, you have to have the opponent's body under control. The old adage is "position before submission." Therefore, all submissions follow rather simply from pins, the guard, or other positions of control, and they are not difficult to describe or to learn. The hard part about them is actually making them work on a resisting opponent who is fighting back, the most difficult part of everything concerned with MMA. Therefore, endless amounts of grappling are required to actually be able to make these things work against another skilled competitor in a match.

REAR NAKED CHOKE

From a solid back control, insert your right elbow crook under your adversary's jaw. You can wedge it in by starting with the sharp part of your forearm. You might need to pull back your opponent's head with your left forearm in order to force his chin to lift up for your right arm to wedge in. When it is wedged in, grab your left biceps with your right hand and cup your left hand over the top back of your adversary's head. Squeeze everything in tight while continuing your lower body pressure, pulling back with your legs and pressing forward with your hips. Whether you are executing this submission face down or face up makes no difference, it is done the same way: take the back and apply the choke.

To defend against this move, you need to get two of your hands on your opponent's choking forearm and pull it down so that it cannot choke you, while at the same time getting your chin down in the way of that same forearm. After generating this bit of safety space, you need to try as hard as you can to spin your whole body around to face your assailant. It can be very tiring and difficult to attempt to strangle a good grappler, so the defender can sometimes patiently wait until the attacker tires, and then be able to power around, spinning to face the choker. Attempting a choke is often more tiring for the choker than it is for the one fighting it off.

Rear Naked Choke

TRIANGLE CHOKE

This is a very common move that works very well against almost anyone. When someone is in your guard, pull his right arm across you so that it is more or less to your right, either held tightly with your hands or clamped against you under your right arm.

You may need to shrimp your hips around in tricky ways to catch a skilled grappler's arm like this. You need to also get your right leg over your opponent's left shoulder so that you can catch the back of his neck in the crook of your knee. Next, hook the top of your right ankle under the crook of your left knee.

Pull your adversary's neck and therefore entire upper body crushingly into you by squeezing your legs in together. This ought to press and trap his right arm against your chest. Now use both your hands to pull your opponent's head down toward you while continuing to squeeze your legs in together. This will induce either a tap out or unconsciousness.

Triangle Choke, Part 1: Setup
Mickey gets one leg over Adam's head.

Triangle Choke, Part 2: Setting Legs
Both legs are in place now.

Triangle Choke, Part 3: Pulling Head
Mickey pulls down Adam's head.

To defend against this attack, you need to avoid getting your arm trapped across your opponent's body and to prevent your adversary from getting his knee crook over your shoulder and onto the back of your neck. As always, to get good at both attack and defense for this move, you need to do lots of grappling. There is no easy or simple way about it.

HAND TRIANGLE

From a scarf hold, with say your right arm around your opponent's neck, you take his right upper arm in your left hand and force the whole arm over to your right across your adversary's face.

Having done this, press your right shoulder and face hard against his right arm and face and join your hands together to increase the pressure.

Hand Triangle, Part 1
Mickey forces Adam's arm into place.

Hand Triangle, Part 2
Mickey completes the choke.

Also, shift your legs so that your right knee is pressing into your opponent's right kidney area and your left leg is straight out behind you, knee off the ground, pushing into the hold with the ball of your left foot. This position generates the same kind of choke as the triangle choke, but it uses your arms instead of your legs as the major players. By applying pressure to your opponent, you can achieve a submission or unconsciousness through strangulation.

To defend against this submission move, do not allow your arm to be pressed across your face if you are held with the scarf hold. *And get out of the scarf hold!*

ARMBAR

This is another very common winning move. From virtually any position, take your opponent's right wrist in your two hands and trap his upper arm between your inner thighs while placing your calves across his chest, allowing your feet to be pushing around the other side of your opponent's ribs.

Getting all this gripping in very tight is critical to making this move work. It does not matter what position you are in, whether you are both face up or face down, as long as you get this grip in, it can work fine. You can even have slight variants on this position. Your left leg might be pressing into your opponent's throat, and your right shin might be pushing into your opponent's right flank. You might even have one of your legs between his. It still might work. Next, pull back on the wrist and thrust upward with your hips, putting extreme pressure on your opponent's elbow joint.

You might have to pull the wrist a little over to the left side rather than straight back depending on your exact position, but

Armbar, Part 1

it makes little difference. As long as you are putting pressure against the normal movement of your adversary's elbow, you can make this work. You will score a tap out with this move. You can just as easily perform this attack on the left wrist, of course, mirroring all the movements described here.

To defend against this submission attempt, get both of your hands together and then spin your body. So if your opponent has your right arm all grappled up, try to attach it to your left hand in some way, and while pulling them in together tightly, spin right in order to face your adversary. Normally there are two ways this happens. Either you join your hands together both between his legs, or you join your left hand to your right making a necklace around your opponent's left thigh. One way or the other, spin your lower body around with your upper body. This renders the armlock ineffective. If you execute this escape when your opponent has his back to the ground, you can even get to a top position, either into his guard, having both your arms inside his legs, or into a side mount position, getting around the outside of his left thigh and then applying a hold down.

Armbar, Part 2

OMOPLATA

This technique is named after the Portuguese word for "shoulder blade," which is the part of the body you appear to be attacking. With your opponent inside your guard and your right calf pressed relatively high on his back, grab a firm hold of his right wrist with your hands and place it against the outside of your left hip.

Next, keeping a grip on the wrist, rotate your hips to the right so that you can get your left calf over your opponent's head and place your left knee crook over his right shoulder. Now you are both facing the same way. Press down on the shoulder with your left leg while pressing forward with your hips.

You will need to release your grip on your opponent's wrist at this point in order to free up your hands for their next duties. Use your belly, hips, and left leg to make sure the arm does not get out. Have your left arm press down on your opponent's back to stop him from rolling over and out of the hold. You can do with your right what the situation demands.

Continue to pull with the left leg while pressing forward with the hips and down with the left arm. This will induce the submission.

Omoplata, Part 1: Trapping the Arm

To get out of an omoplata, you have to roll forward. But better than having to roll out of an omoplata and likely ending in a compromising position underneath your adversary, try to avoid getting put into it in the first place. Do not allow your opponent to pull your wrist down outside his hip, and do not let him get his leg over your shoulder. Grapple a lot!

Omoplata, Part 2: Getting the Leg into Position

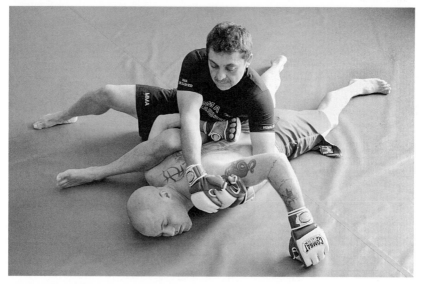

Omoplata, Part 3: Completing the Submission

KIMURA

This submission is named for the legendary judo champion Masahiko Kimura. It works just as well in a no *gi* situation such as the kind we are treating in this book as it does in a judo tourney. With your opponent in your guard, grab his right wrist with both of your hands and control it.

Next, keeping a very strong hold on the wrist with your left hand, release your right in order to overhook his right upper arm. Try to hug it firmly under your right armpit. Now, from this new overhooking position, grab either your left wrist or your opponent's right wrist with your right hand and, while keeping tight pressure with your armpit, rotate your opponent's right wrist up and away from you, making the armlock happen.

For defense, if you get your wrist caught in the initial stages of a Kimura, do various things to stop it from being fully controlled, such as join your two hands together, hitting your opponent's face with the other hand, and so on. The most important thing is to free the wrist from your adversary's grip.

Kimura, Part 1: Trapping the Arm

Kimura, Part 2: Getting the Tap Out

AMERICANA

From a side mount where your legs are to your opponent's right side, grab your opponent's left wrist with your left arm and place your left elbow to the left of his head.

This should create a kind of square angle out of your adversary's left arm. Next, weave your right hand under your opponent's upper arm and grip your right hand over your left hand or wrist. Then push his left wrist in the direction of his left hip while cranking up with your right elbow.

This submission can also be done in reverse fashion, by taking your opponent's left wrist in your right hand, sticking your right elbow outside of his left waist area, and weaving your left hand under his upper arm and onto your right hand or his left wrist. In this case, you aim to press his left wrist toward his head, while cranking up with your left elbow.

Americana, Part 1: Trapping the Arm

Americana, Part 2: Achieving the Tap Out

If the opponent straightens out his arm to prevent you from finishing the cranking motion, you can actually complete the submission all the same by continuing to crank and press. The move can be applied even when your opponent's arm is quite straight. The twisting and pressing makes it work one way or the other. Just be sure that everything is tight and that you are continuing to pin him with the rest of your body.

SCARF LOCK

From a scarf hold where you have, for example, your right arm around your opponent's neck, take his right wrist in your left hand, shove his right upper arm over your right thigh, and put his right wrist under your right knee area.

Next, squeeze your calf into his right forearm so his wrist cannot escape out from under your leg, and lift your hips off the ground while pulling in the opposite direction with your right leg to keep everything tight. This makes the armlock work.

It is also possible to make this move effective even if you cannot force your opponent's wrist under your leg. As long as you get his right upper arm over your right thigh, you can win

Scarf Lock, Part 1
Mickey forces Chris's arm into place under his leg.

Scarf Lock, Part 2
Mickey lifts his hips to get the tap out.

by catching his forearm in the crook of your left knee and using the strength of your left arm and leg to strain your opponent's elbow over your right thigh, inducing a submission.

For defense, the main thing, if caught in the scarf hold, is to get your right elbow onto the floor so that your upper arm cannot be hauled over your opponent's thigh. If you keep your elbow on the floor, you can even start to escape from the pin itself.

GUILLOTINE

This is one of the most common submission techniques found in ancient artwork. It is somewhat unique amongst submission techniques because it can be done fairly easily while standing up.

Its modern name comes from the French instrument of death. The guillotine can be done either standing or on the ground. A common method for doing it while standing is to get the back of your opponent's neck under your right armpit. Wedge your right forearm under his chin and up into his throat. Join your hands together, squeeze everything in tightly, and lift your forearm up. If you are doing this move on the ground, or are going to the ground, you need to get your legs into the closed guard position and make everything tight.

Against an experienced grappler, this technique can be hard to make work. To defend against the guillo-

Guillotine Standing

Guillotine in Guard

tine, after having your head locked in, press your head forward as if wanting to put it even farther through the hold and out the other side. Break your adversary's hand grip by placing one or both of your hands on his and pulling down. Peel the forearm out too, by pulling down on the wrist of that arm. When your head is free, you can get it out and keep fighting.

LEGLOCKS

Leglocks can be relatively hard to execute due to the great strength of the legs. You may have noticed that in most submission techniques, you are using several strong body parts, like legs, hips, and arms, to attack a weak body part like the neck or one arm. In *gi* events, the friction of the *gi* allows for some leglocks to work fairly well as they catch and trap the leg. In MMA, where we are dealing with slippery individuals in shorts, it is rather hard to trap the leg. But there are two very effective leglocks that can be used.

One, the kneebar, is done very much like the basic armlock described above. From any facing direction, up, down, or sideways, grip your opponent's ankle in your hands. Next, while stretching and straightening the leg out as much as is possible,

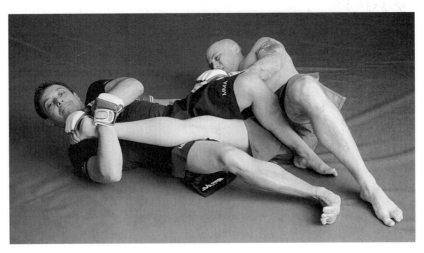

Kneebar
Mickey (in black) submits Adam.

sit on the knee area, placing your calves under his thigh or hips, crossing them if you like and making everything tight. Next, pull back on the ankle with your arms, and if you like, grip it even more tightly in a hug. Then press forward with your hips while pulling back with your arms and legs. A good entry to this is where you are standing up inside your opponent's guard and you trap an ankle that he has raised up. You can then spin in for the move.

The other good leglock for mixed martial arts is the heel hook. You are in your adversary's guard. Trap his, say, left foot under your right armpit and apply the same hand technique as for the guillotine choke, but to the ankle. Then squeeze your thighs around the leg and use your feet to press his hips down into the floor. You might even be able to get a submission out of this position if you can force the ridge of your forearm hard enough into your adversary's Achilles tendon. However, more likely you will have to finish the technique with the heel hook. To make it work, simply change your hand position. Cradle the right side of your opponent's left heel in the crook of your right

Heel Hook
Mickey makes Adam tap.

elbow and join your hands together over top of his ankle. Keeping everything tight, rotate your adversary's heel counterclockwise. This completes the maneuver and enables you to get the tap out.

The "Language" of MMA

All the moves from this and the previous chapter form the standard vocabulary of MMA, the next chapter on strategies and tactics is the grammar, and the final chapters on sparring and competing are where everything comes together as real language. This is a metaphor, but a helpful one. Just knowing how to perform the moves in the skills chapters is not enough. You have to use these moves strategically and train in changing and fully resisting, competitive environments to make them effective fighting moves. However, do not move on to the chapters on strategy and sparring until you fully understand and can practice what is contained in the skills chapters.

TACTICS AND STRATEGIES

This chapter links the skills you learned in the previous chapters. Starting with an initial position, we will look at how it can morph into others and what to do along the way to make sure you have the greatest possible advantage at each stage of the game. The drills described here are designed to develop your sense of what to use and when, in the most common and most precarious situations. This chapter is meant to be read through over and over again during your training so that you can apply it to your sparring and fighting. To learn how to use this information to good effect, work through the progressions with your coach and training partners, on the mats. Assiduously practice the drills. As the famous combat athlete Aristocles, known to posterity by his ring name "Plato," the "Broad One," wrote, "You need to make your training as much like the real thing as possible for it to be effective." This means lots of fighting it out from as many key positions as possible. Sparring only with the same group of training partners gets you into a comfort zone where you tend to overtrain certain positions as fight patterns develop. This is why live drilling is so important. You cannot fully anticipate what positions you will end up in while fighting in the cage, so you have to be prepared for all of them.

Regarding striking, sparring with partners will give you positional control and accuracy, but it will weaken your power because you have to take care not to harm your partners. This is why there is no substitute for focus mitts and pads drills. While doing them you have to hit at full speed and power at all the angles and positions of a real match. Situational sparring drills and focus pad and mitt work are all excellent ways to overcome the limitations of your own group of training partners and coaches and develop your fighting-specific toughness, power, speed, stamina, and strength.

The Importance of Upright Wrestling

The base skills of MMA are those of keeping your balance in the clinch and keeping your opponent off balance there. You can knee, elbow, punch, and throw an unbalanced adversary in the clinch, and you can prevent him doing the same to you by keeping yourself balanced and in control of the grips. Conversely, if your antagonist knocks you off balance in the clinch, you will be put in the position of having to defend yourself or escape from those same elbows, punches, and throws. Whether it's your strategy to keep the fight standing, take the fight to the ground, or keep the fight in the clinch so you can strike from there, you have to be good at wrestling in the clinch. Solid upright wrestling skills are what allow you to control a fight. Upright wrestling drills are therefore perfect for developing the ability to control the clinch. From this base of upright wrestling, you need to expand your skills outward in two directions. One direction leads to skills involving more and more distance between yourself and your opponent: first to striking in the clinch, then to boxing, and finally to kicking. Another direction leads to the ground: striking through guard, passing guard, pinning and mounting, hitting, and submitting. We start by examining the mounted position on the ground and then expand outward from it all the way to free kicking standing up.

Full Mount

Is there anything more synonymous with MMA than the full mount? This is the defining move of mixed martial arts. To the uninitiated, it looks like a barbaric "beat down," but it is in fact a position of great tactical and strategic complexity. It is of course the ultimate position for winning in MMA, akin to threatening checkmate in chess. But why is this so?

To begin with, you are pinning your opponent across the chest, sitting on him actually, with your legs providing support to both sides to stop you from being tipped off either to the right or to the left. The person being pinned has no way to effectively stop your powerful punches from being rained down upon his face, a very brittle part of the body: cheekbones and noses are both terrifically vulnerable here. The floor underneath the back of the head provides no give, making the strikes to the face that much more devastating. You have gravity on your side as well as mobility to "wind up" your punches. While the bottom person can still put up some resistance to the beating, his disadvantage is so great that you will end up scoring a tap or knockout if he cannot escape in time.

If you are the one on top, you need to keep your opponent pinned and yourself from being tossed off. Your strategy involves focusing on several things:

1. Remain stable in the "saddle" by being ready to stretch out either leg to provide a better brace against rolling than your knee can afford if you are being rolled to either side. If your opponent rolls to his left, you must counter by extending your right leg, being fully prepared to shift legs if your opponent rolls the other way. You need to do the same thing if your opponent is trying to trap your ankle into his side to start rolling you off: be sure to extend your leg on that side far enough out that he will not be able to trap it in. Beware also of your opponent trying to scoot his arms and head right under you and out the back. This is prevented by not allowing his arms to get under your hips.

2. Following the old adage of "The best defense is a good offense," don't allow your opponent to think of anything besides his immediate safety. Keep a steady flow of punches coming to your adversary. If

you let up for an instant, this gives your opponent a chance to start an escape and postpones your chance at victory.

3. Keep your head and torso up. If you bow down to effect a grappling-style pin, you deny yourself the necessary space to deliver strikes, and even worse, your opponent can tire you out and even start to get away by clamping your head down, encircling your neck and upper back with his arms.

4. You can look for the opportunity to effect a basic armlock when your antagonist stretches out one of his arms straight while trying to stop your hits. If you are sure you can pull this move off, you can win with it immediately. If you are not sure, then stick to your striking strategy.

5. If your adversary manages to pop you up a bit and turn over to his hands and knees in turtle position, besides hitting his head, you can also try to take back control by getting your hooks in. You normally have to get one hook in at a time. Using your heel, force your foot between your opponent's knee and arm. Sometimes this requires some effort because an intelligent opponent will be trying to thwart your attempts. Once a bit of space is achieved, force your foot into the opening and place your leg inside your opponent's inner thigh. Then do the same for the other leg. Keep your heels digging into your opponent's groin area and your hips pressing forward. If you let up your pressure, your opponent can begin to escape. If you are lucky, you may be able to flatten your opponent when you get your hooks in. This is a difficult position to get out of, as your opponent cannot move his legs; they may actually be high in the air. It is a horrible situation for your opponent and terrifically difficult to reverse. Do not cross your legs or you can get leglocked by your opponent pressing down on them with his own legs. From here you can attempt a rear naked choke.

If you are on the bottom of a full mount, you are of course in, for lack of a better way of putting it, the worst position possible. Things, however, are not necessarily entirely hopeless. There are some things you can try to do.

BLOCKING

First of all, you have to make sure you don't get knocked out. This is difficult to prevent, but obviously getting your hands up to block will be a first step. It is important to remember to keep your arms flexed and not straight in order to avoid an armlock. A good second step is to pull your opponent's arms, head, and upper body down into you so he can't punch you anymore. Just as you were cautious to avoid denying yourself room to strike when you were on top, here you can be aggressive by trying to take striking room away from your opponent.

Unfortunately, unless the bell is about to go off signaling the end of a round, merely attempting to block the strikes of your opponent from beneath a full mount will only delay the inevitable, and sooner or later you will succumb to his efforts and lose the match. Therefore, your only hope is to actually get out of the pin.

Escaping a Mount

TRAP AND ROLL

If your opponent is unsteady, you can suddenly pop your hips up and hope he flies off and you can scoot out to one side or the other or, more spectacularly, right between his legs. A skilled opponent, however, will not simply go soaring off like a bird for you. So try to tie up one of his arms either by clamping it under one of your armpits or by grabbing it tightly at the wrist. To pop your hips up, bring your feet as close under your hips as you can and flat on the floor. Then thrust your hips up. Rise up on your toes when you pop your hips to give the move greater leverage.

Part 2 of the escape is to trap your antagonist's leg on the same side as the arm you have already captured. You do this by simply placing your foot over the top of his and setting it down tightly against the outside of his ankle. If you can't visualize this, then just get in the position and try it. You will now notice that

Trap and Roll (Front View)
Mickey (on the bottom) traps Chris's right arm
and leg.

you have both his arm and his leg on that side pulled in snugly against your body. It is almost effortless now for you to roll over toward that same side. You will end up inside your opponent's guard. Now you have a slight advantage in the fight rather than being on the threshold of defeat, as you were only a moment before. Keep in mind that your opponent will be actively trying to stop you from trapping his ankles and arms, so you have to be deft and clever to dupe him into letting you tie them up like this and roll him over.

Trap and Roll (Side View)
Mickey (in black) traps Chris's right arm and leg.

TURTLE

If you can't escape by popping your hips, and there is too much time left to just try to stall, you are in a very bad way. At this time you might consider a more desperate attempt to get out by turtling yourself. Turtling is very risky because it makes you vulnerable to the rear naked choke and keeps you in great danger of blows to the head. But it can be an improvement over being in a full mount if you play it right or if the rules do not allow your opponent to strike your head from behind. This more flustered attempt to get out of a full mount is to simply pop your hips up to get some space and turn over from lying on your back to crouching on your hands and knees. Crouching like this is called turtling. *Do not* turn over to lie flat on your belly though. In MMA, you will most certainly be beaten to a pulp. Also, under no circumstances allow your opponent to wrap his heels into your inner thighs, as discussed earlier from the offensive perspective. This is called "getting his hooks in." If your adversary gets his hooks in, he can flatten you out and strangle you with the rear naked choke.

ROLLING

If you are hooked, rather than resigning yourself to this vulnerable position, your best option might be to roll. Your adversary will still have taken your back with your legs clamped, but at least you will open yourself up to better options. Rolling is a viable strategy if your opponent gets his hooks in while you are kneeling. As the name implies, simply roll so that you are on top of your opponent. In this position, you will both be facing the sky while your opponent has his chest pressed against your back, his hooks still in place.

Your immediate priority from this new position is to defend yourself against a possible choke, as this will most likely be your opponent's most convenient attack. To do so, grab hold of the wrist that your opponent is trying to choke you with and lean your body to that side. Your opponent will of course be trying

Rear Naked Choke Defense, Part 1
Chris (in white) defends Adam's choke attempt.

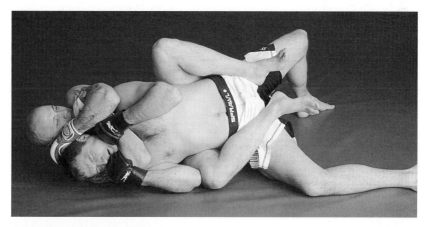

Rear Naked Choke Defense, Part 2
Chris rolls to the side of Adam's choking arm, relieving the choke by using the ground to press up on Adam's arm.

to stop you from doing that, but if you successfully immobilize his arm you will be able to stall his choke attempt. The reason the move works is because your adversary's choking arm will be trapped against the ground, held by both your arms. It is stuck; he cannot move it to squeeze your neck any tighter.

From here, keeping a tight grip on your opponent's bottom choking arm with your bottom arm, use your higher arm to peel off your antagonist's ankle from out of your inner thigh on that side. So, let us say you are being held with your opponent's right arm under your chin and digging into your throat, and you lean to the right, keeping hold of his right arm with your two hands. You would let go your grip of your adversary's arm with your left hand and then use it to peel out his left heel from your left inner thigh.

Once your opponent's left heel is out of the picture, you can immediately spin over clockwise to your right and end up face down on top of your adversary, pinning him. Because your antagonist's heel was pulled out, there is nothing stopping you from rotating over and out.

Rear Naked Choke Defense, Part 3
Chris peels out Adam's left leg and prepares to spin over and pin him.

LEGLOCK DEFENSE

It is possible to leglock an opponent who is attempting the rear naked choke on you if he crosses his legs. Your response is to simply overhook his top leg with one of yours and place your other leg on top of your first leg to add pressure to the leglock. So, for example, if your opponent has your back in back control with hooks in and crosses his right leg over his left, quickly overhook his right leg with your right leg, place your left calf or ankle over top of your right shin or ankle, and press down. You can get a swift submission with this move and win the entire match with this little trick!

Of course, a skillful grappler should know not to cross his legs while taking your back, and it would be difficult to force him to. You are much better off trying to escape from the back control as described previously, but if your opponent does make a mistake, it's up to you to make sure he pays for it. Interestingly, a person with thick legs can do a one-legged ankle lock on an opponent regardless of whether he crosses his legs. With strong legs, only one leg is needed to overhook the ankle and apply the pressure.

Back Control Leglock Retaliation
Adam (on top) is about to make Chris (on the bottom) tap.

STANDING UP

If, when you first turtled yourself and rolled over to your hands and knees, you were able to avoid your adversary's getting his hooks in, you stand a good chance of being able to stand right up. Being on your hands and knees can be disastrous for you if you stay there, but if you turtle for only an instant in order to stabilize your body for getting back up onto your feet, it can be a very good thing! While an opponent who is only grappling and not striking you will likely be able to keep your turtle pressed down and prevent you from rising, one who is winding up to hit you with arms and knees will generate space that you can take advantage of to stand up. This is why in all wrestling and grappling styles around the world that continue the fight on the ground, including Brazilian Jiu-Jitsu, judo, and freestyle wrestling, the turtle without hooks in is not considered a pin: it is too easy to get back up to your feet from it.

While your head is more vulnerable to strikes in the turtle than in a back down pin, you have the chance to immediately get back up to your feet from the turtle and retaliate, whereas from a back down pin you do not; you are quite stuck. Even though in a back down pin you have your arms to provide a modicum of defense against your antagonist's hits, you are trapped, so eventually you will get knocked out. In turtle you might escape very quickly, before getting hit in the first place or after taking only one or two shots. It is even possible to throw your opponent with a leg grab throw like the double leg takedown if you manage to tackle his legs. However, for the purposes of MMA, think of the turtle as a pin and a bad place to be, although it is better than being fully mounted and has a few options available to get back up to your feet quickly.

SHOULDER THROW AND WINDING THROW

If you can't stand up because your antagonist is straddling you and has wrapped one of his arms over or under your shoulder, you can grab hold of that arm with your arms and effect a shoulder throw or winding throw. Let us say your opponent is straddling you in a back mount and has wrapped his right arm over or under your right shoulder, clamping you in tight and preventing you from standing up and getting away. Start out by simply clamping his arm in even more tightly. You are now in the perfect position to perform your shoulder or winding throw. You do this by gluing your right foot tightly to the outside of his right ankle, keeping your opponent's right arm clamped in snugly with your arms, and rolling over to the right side. You will see that in this position on the ground you are free of your opponent's legs entirely, and you are easily able from it to establish a pin of your choice. If you do get caught up between your opponent's legs, execute the same kind of escape you would for the rear naked choke.

Full Mount Drill

It is imperative that you train to handle both the top and bottom positions of the full mount. You have to be able to keep your position on top and win from there if you manage to attain it, and conversely, you have to be able to escape if you happen to be on the bottom. Practice pinning a training partner with the full mount. Make sure you keep your posture upright and do not bend your upper body down as if executing a judo or wrestling pin. Keep your upper body erect and your legs well based on the floor to either side of your partner's flanks or ribs. You will find yourself using both your knees and your feet to keep contact with the floor on both sides, shifting around as necessary to the moment. The drill is for your partner to try to escape from your mount, and it is your duty to prevent him from doing so. Your partner's job is to try to get you off somehow and stand up or even roll on top of you if possible.

When drilling for the escape, grapple it out from the full mount until the bottom person has gotten up to his feet, has established any kind of full or half guard, has gotten to turtle position with no hooks in, or has been able to roll the top fighter over and has landed on top of him chest-to-chest. The top person in this drill only needs to prevent the bottom person from doing any of these things. The top person's job is to maintain either top mount or back control. If the bottom person manages to roll over and turtle, the top fighter must immediately get his hooks in. If the bottom person turtles for as short a time as three seconds without the top fighter's hooks in, then score the round a victory for the bottom player. If the top player maintains top mount or back control for a few minutes, then declare the top fighter the winner. However, if the top player is able to achieve a submission, for example the rear naked choke from back control, even better! Please keep in mind that a back control is valid regardless of whether the one executing it is on top of or underneath his opponent. Make sure you play both sides in this drill so you get good at fighting from the top as well as from the bottom. We stop at the unhooked turtle position in this drill to allow for focus on the mounted position. A separate drill, the *par terre* drill, fully treats the turtle.

This full mount drill also covers the back control position somewhat, and it is an excellent first drill for grappling as it trains you for the ultimate fighting position of MMA. To complement it, you should also sometimes add in light striking, as you will notice is recommended for all the grappling drills you will meet with in this chapter. In each case, spend more time training the grappling because you can put your full strength into the fighting, whereas when you add in light striking you have to go easy and lose realism in terms of power. However, you need to feel how the striking affects your grappling positioning, as it most certainly does.

To develop powerful punches from the full mount position, straddle a heavy bag with a full mount and punch and hammer fist it repeatedly. You will learn how to deliver your strikes with full power this way, whereas with your partner you will have to be gentle and therefore cannot learn how to hit hard.

The full mount is the target position for your fighting. Mounting your opponent gives you a greater chance of winning than any other single position in mixed martial arts. Although you can finish off your opponent with knockout blows or some quick submissions from other positions, the full mount is the most dominant position in this game and should always be a goal in your mind, or at least one of your greatest fears. Because fighting to achieve it can be very difficult against another good grappler, striking all the time is important for both weakening your opponent's resistance and scoring potential knockouts.

Handling the Turtle

There are some caveats though regarding the full mount. If your opponent is turtling, there is no need in MMA for you to try for a full mount. Instead aim to hit him as much as you can with elbows, knees, punches, and hammer fists while keeping him pinned down on all fours with your upper body and forearms. If you feel confident about it, you can get your hooks in, take your opponent's back, and attempt the rear naked choke. If your opponent turtles for you, it is a gift. Being able to prevent a turtler from getting up while you hit him actually takes a lot of grappling practice and skill, so do lots of intense grappling to prepare yourself!

PAR TERRE DRILL

A good way to train yourself to keep an opponent's turtle down and stop him from getting up and away is to wrestle with a partner or your coach from the *par terre* position. This position is where your partner has turtled and you are on top. Your partner is to do everything in his power to get up and away or trap one of your arms or legs and roll you to your back but to not go to his back for any reason. It is your job to try to keep him down in turtle position, submit him, or turn him over to his back. To effect a submission you may want to achieve the back control position, which can lead to interesting tactical work on both players' parts. If you are defending, you will want to ensure your partner does not get his hooks in on you in order to prevent him from taking your back. If the bottom person's back is taken in back control, then fight it out until he gets away or submits. Do not use strikes in this drill for safety in training. On the ground, effective striking most often depends on effective grappling dominance, so grappling comes before striking in your training for ground fighting. You can do this drill at full power because you are not including strikes, and it will do a lot for your ability to grapple. You should play the role of both top and bottom person in this drill to learn how to handle the turtle from both sides. If for some reason you aren't getting into the rear naked choke progression very often, then intentionally start this drill with the hooks in, in back control position. The rear naked choke is a very important move in MMA, one of the most effective grappling finishes there is in the sport.

To complement but not replace this full-out modified classical wrestling drill, also do it with the top person simulating strikes. Gently apply knees, elbows, punches, and hammer fists to the turtling person, particularly to the head, to create the kind of windup space that you will need to generate to hit a turtling opponent in the ring. Now it is harder to keep the turtler down as he has more space to get up and less pressure pushing down on his back.

Fighting Through the Guard

The founders of Brazilian Jiu-Jitsu, the Gracie family, identified the guard position as the one deserving the most study for MMA ground fighting, stemming from their academy's long experience in the *vale tudo* mixed martial arts ring. There is no question that the person on top is in the better position in guard, but there are still a number of tricks available to the bottom fighter, and at the least there are a number of stalling and defensive tactics that the competitor on the bottom can make use of to delay or prevent the top fighter's victory. Based on having the guard as the literal "on guard" position of ground fighting, the way the clinch is for standing wrestling, the *par terre* is for ground wrestling, and the "on guard" stance is for boxing and fencing, the Gracie family developed a new and unique grappling sport, Brazilian Jiu-Jitsu, in the 1970s. Its purpose is aligned as closely as ground grappling can be with the grappling progressions needed for success in mixed martial arts fights. The aim in Brazilian Jiu-Jitsu, as it often is in MMA, is to pass the guard into full mount if you are the top person, and to effect a sweep and end up on top in full mount, or simply scoot out and stand up, if you are the bottom person. As pointed out, the top position is preferred, so skillful wrestling is needed to attempt to gain the top position first before entering into guard play. Both Brazilian Jiu-Jitsu and MMA fights must normally pass through the critical clinch stage where the throwing skills of wrestling and judo determine who will achieve top position in guard on the ground, or even end up past the opponent's guard on the ground.

The most useful individual techniques of guard fighting are outlined in the skills chapters of this book. What we must now do is learn to put them together in sequence.

ON TOP IN GUARD

If you are able to get up to your feet in a wide and stable stance and deliver effective punches and hammer fists to your opponent's face, this is the first thing to try when you are in your antagonist's guard. It is possible to wear out your opponent with this, and even score a knockout at some point. However, there are many variables that affect how good a strategy this is. If you are facing a very skillful grappler, you might have your ankle hooked with his elbow crook and find yourself pushed backward down into the ground with the handstand sweep. You might find it hard to stand up due to fatigue or skillful attempts to unbalance you from below. You even might find it difficult to land effective blows due to practiced and energetic defense. Therefore, you need to be able to pass guard, or at least constantly threaten to, to put your adversary on the defensive rather than the offensive. You will want to pass guard even if you are scoring with your hits because you can score even more when closer to your opponent's face in full mount!

The first thing to do in an opponent's guard is make sure your posture is erect and you are well balanced. This is called having good base. If you are kneeling and need to brace your arms against something or keep your opponent pressed down, push your palm or palms heavily into your adversary's belly, and no higher up on his body than that. Doing this pins his hips down for you. You want to make it hard for your antagonist to move around underneath you. You need to stop him from swiveling his hips around and catching you with a submission. You want to frustrate him and tire him out. If you can keep your adversary stuck in one place under you, then you are the one in control, and you can focus on attacking rather than defending.

Even though you have erect posture, remember to avoid armlocks by keeping your arms bent. If your palms are positioned higher than advised, your upper body will begin to bend forward, making you vulnerable for sweeps, submissions, and even strikes with the fist and elbow. With your upper body closer to your opponent's, he can try to pull you down to start sweep and submission attempts. Whether you are passing guard or striking through guard, keep an upright posture. If you are standing and your opponent is lying down in guard waiting for you, you have the option of disengaging and insisting that your opponent get up and fight on his feet.

In grappling tourneys you have to pass guard, and techniques involving grabbing the legs are often employed for this.

These can work in MMA too if you can avoid getting kicked in the face or head, but striking through guard is often a good choice because it is less risky. Do not feel, however, that you always have to pass guard. It is a goal to have, but both "ground and pound" and disengaging to force the fight back up can be legitimate strategies as well. In these respects MMA guard tactics can differ significantly from those of grappling matches.

If you are inside an opponent's butterfly guard, in a no *gi* MMA environment there is nothing keeping you down pressing into him, since you are not being gripped and kept pulled in. To get over a butterfly guard, you might consider the hop over pass, or simply disengaging, if your strikes are having no effect. If you disengage, you can force the fight back up to standing. It is quite easy to disengage from a butterfly guard in no *gi* MMA. The butterfly guard is a particularly good guard for someone well practiced in grappling because it is much easier to sweep someone over from it than from the basic guard. Both feet are under the adversary's groin, quite ready to pick him right up. Beware of getting swept if you are inside someone's butterfly guard!

ON THE BOTTOM IN GUARD

If you are on the bottom in guard, it means that you have most likely lost the clinch phase of the fight and have been thrown down to the ground, but you have been able to establish guard there to prevent your opponent from getting right on top of you for a pin. It is not good to be on the bottom in guard in MMA or BJJ tourneys, as it is the weaker position. Therefore you must play your cards wisely. There are several submissions available for you to use from the guard, and several sweeps also. You might even be able to punch and elbow the head of an opponent who is in your guard.

To establish guard, simply shift your hips so that you can stretch one leg around your opponent's trunk on one side and your other leg around the other side. You will often have to pivot on your hips to do this. This kind of skill comes from doing lots of grappling. Its concept is easy, like throwing a ball, but getting quick, strong, and effective with it takes time, just as throwing a ball does. If your aim is to achieve butterfly guard then you must place your legs accordingly; it is a little trickier than attaining the basic guard but well worth getting good at as it is a more aggressive guard than the basic one is.

Handstand Sweep. This is a good sweep for an opponent standing up in your

Handstand Sweep, Part 1
Chris has hooked Adam's leg with his right arm and leg.

Handstand Sweep, Part 2
Chris forces Adam to the ground and prepares to take a top position.

basic guard. If your opponent is standing up and striking at you, you can shift your hips so as to hook the elbow crook of one of your arms behind his ankle and push your antagonist down backward with your legs and hips.

GUARD DRILL

There's no way to get around the fact that to get good at fighting you must spend a lot of time actually fighting. The moderating factor is that real fighting is very hard on your body, so you need to approximate your practice fighting as closely to real fighting as possible, but at the same time minimize the wear and tear on yourself as much as you can. To learn how to handle the guard, you need to practice fighting from it as both top person and bottom person.

To do the guard drill, start in the guard position. Since there are two major kinds of guard, train both of them, basic and butterfly. Refer to Chapter 3 to refresh yourself on the basics of each. Using only grappling and no striking skills, the top partner must try to pass the bottom player's guard and establish some kind of pin, such as a scarf hold, knee on belly, side mount, north-south, full mount, or even back control, for at least three seconds. The bottom player's objectives are to sweep the top person over and end up in full mount or another pin, or have the top fighter submit through a choke or joint lock. If the top player passes the guard momentarily, as long as the bottom person can reestablish guard before being pinned for three seconds, the fight continues. A guard pass is only a legitimate pass if it ends in a pin. Just is in the *par terre* drill, it is imperative that you play both top and bottom roles.

As with the *par terre* drill, you should complement the guard drill with a period of light striking. It is important not to hurt your training partners, or they cannot train with you. The point of adding in light striking to this exercise is to get you used to how striking affects your and your opponent's positioning in the guard fighting. Because the drill it is not full powered, it cannot ever replace the full-out grappling drill, but it is very important to do all the same. While doing the guard drill with light striking, attempt all the passes and sweeps you normally would while playing top or bottom, but try to do them while striking. You will learn a lot from this drill. Do not just try to hit; try to pass or sweep as well.

GROUND AND POUND DRILL

For this drill, the top person is in the other person's guard. Again, train both major kinds of guard, but also train in the half guard on both sides. Ground and pound can be a fight ender, so give it the necessary time in your training to become proficient at it. In this drill the top fighter is not trying to pass guard but is rather only trying to score hits, primarily to the bottom player's face. The bottom player, however, is trying to get back to his feet, sweep or submit the top person, and even to hit back. Of course the bottom fighter has to try to avoid getting hit by blocking and moving around. It is important to be gentle with each other in this drill.

To practice hitting full power in these positions, lay a heavy bag on the floor, adopt the kind of positions you would inside an opponent's guard, such as being in a wide stance or kneeling, and hit the bag where an opponent's face would be relative to you. Deliver

Punching Through Guard

punches and hammer fists especially. At first this will seem very awkward, and especially tiring for your legs, but after a while you will condition yourself and ultimately help your overall fighting prowess.

Getting to the Ground

We have described how to win on the ground. In every case, one person is on top and the other on the bottom. While the bottom fighter can reverse his position and end up on top, it is much better to end up on top right from the start of the ground fighting phase of combat, because the top fighter has the decided advantage. This section deals with how to go from standing up and clinching to a top position on the ground. Clinch fighting has been particularly the domain of judo and wrestling, but also of Muay Thai in recent combat sport history.

As pointed out earlier in this book, if you cannot take your opponent down, you cannot be sure you can use any of your ground fighting techniques. If you cannot defend against getting taken down, you cannot use your kickboxing skills to any good effect. Mixed martial arts athletes who overspecialize in either kickboxing or grappling without getting good at judo and wrestling skills in the clinch have often come up short in matches. Strange to say, if one had to choose which of the two extremes, ground grappling or kickboxing, to become proficient at, ground grappling is the better choice because a grappler can hang on to a kickboxer and pull both down together and then apply a submission technique on the ground.

However, when clinch work is well developed on both sides, the fight will tend to go to the better kickboxer, who can score more hits while keeping the fight standing. The logic behind this is simple. The kickboxer with good clinch work can hit well on his feet and can also avoid getting taken down. A grappler facing this kind of opponent will often not be able to take the fight to the ground because the wrestling in the clinch will be mixed in with annoying punches, knees, elbows, and kicks, so he will have to stay standing up and will get hit a lot. The kickboxer-wrestler can insist on keeping the fight standing, but the grappler-wrestler will likely not be able to bring the fight to the ground, providing the other person's takedown defense skills are reasonably good. In MMA, you must get up on your feet and fight. Lying on the ground waiting for your opponent to jump on you so you can submit him is noncombative (in addition to being boring for the spectators) and therefore is not allowed. Two skilled wrestlers or judoka will find their skills canceling each other out to a large degree, and both will find it hard to achieve anything more than a stalemate in the clinch; both will often remain standing. Therefore weakening and even knocking out or otherwise incapacitating the opponent with strikes is crucial for achieving victory but is all for naught without good judo or wrestling skills for handling the clinch. For this reason, we will start by detailing how to take an opponent down and defend against a takedown, and then once these are understood we can add in strikes.

When Jigoro Kano created judo in 1882, he intentionally mixed together traditional samurai Jiu-Jitsu skills with Western wrestling rules and techniques. His objective was to create a sport that would double as a hand-to-hand fighting art. For safety reasons, he banned striking from his competitions, and he quickly noticed a problem: the athletes would fight in bent-over postures. He was quite upset about this and remarked that while the bent-over posture helps to provide some defense in a grappling match, in real fighting it invites getting beat up with strikes. He banned leg grabs for this reason, although they were reintroduced to judo after his death. The traditional French wrestling style, called *Greco-Roman* because its origins are thought to lie back in ancient times in Roman Gaul (the ancient name for France), has always banned leg grabs, and this rule likely reflects this style's battlefield origins. The same logic goes for mixed martial arts competitions. While it is often an excellent tactic to drop low in order to score a leg grab throw such as the single or double leg throw, it is something that needs to be done swiftly; it is not a good plan to remain low for extended periods of time. Bending over makes you vulnerable to being pushed down, kneed in the face, or hit on the head. Keep this in mind as you train for handling the clinch.

Unlike ground fighting, the clinch does not really have progressions to work through. The closest things to progressions in upright wrestling are the grips outlined in the skills chapters. They are the double and single overhook, over-under, double underhook, and leg grabs. Certain neutral grips are often employed while fighting for dominance, such as a single overhook and elbow crook grip, often called the collar and elbow grip.

As mentioned earlier, athletes tend to find themselves in an over-under situation a lot because it is even for the two players. They allow each other to keep this grip because it is not especially fearsome to defend against, nor is it particularly bad for offense. This fact is borne out not only by wrestlers around the world but also by judo players who most commonly adopt a collar and elbow grip on the *gi* when fighting, the *gi* equivalent of the over-under grip.

The double underhook is the strongest wrestling grip, but it requires good lifting strength in your arms and whole body. Unless you have developed good strength for this, you will find it very difficult to wrestle. Weight lifting is highly recommended. In particular, grip strength is very important, and this can be developed through weight lifting also. Dead lifts, curls, rows, the clean and jerk, and so on, any kind of weight lifting exercise involving gripping and moving weights, can help develop the raw strength and power for the double underhook grip and for wrestling and judo in general. All of this applies equally to the clinch fighting stage of MMA. One defensive strategy that can be used against an opponent who is double underhooking you is to squeeze your arms together, which can prevent him from getting in close enough to perform a throw.

When trying to throw an opponent, you cannot expect to try only a single move and have it work. You need to attack with a combination of at least two moves. Exactly which two you use has to vary from match to match, since you do not want to become predictable. Therefore, practice many different combinations and get good at them. One basic concept is to change the angle of attack when shifting from one throw attempt to another. Therefore, if your first throw attacks left, be prepared to have your second throw attack straight through or right, switch from high to low throws like a leg hook throw to a single leg throw, and so on. All of this is not to say that your first throw attempt will never work, but you need to perform it and each subsequent throw at full power, readying yourself for a third and even a fourth throw attempt if necessary. There is really no rule about which combinations are best. Since this sport is all about confusing your opponent into not knowing how to defend your next attack, what combinations will actually work will depend on whom you are fighting, your own body shape and size relative to his, your relative levels of skill or fatigue, and so on. An initial throw attempt can disorient your opponent enough for you to at least progress to a stronger grip. Be able to do all the throws, and be skilled at using all of them. Thinking that certain combinations are written in stone and focusing only on them will weaken your game.

Once you are good at wrestling in the clinch, you can start to include strikes into your game plan. Strikes change things up, but they do not make the wrestling skills any less valuable. Do not expect to strike in the clinch or be able to disengage in order to strike your opponent without being an expert at wrestling first. If your wrestling or judo skills are weak, you will either get tossed to the ground or slip up and fall down because of your poor balance and end up on your butt defending yourself. The part of the fight spent in the clinch may not always last very long, but it is the most volatile and critical point of the match. Master it! If you cannot handle the clinch, then get out of the ring.

The only way to actually get good at wrestling in the clinch is to wrestle in the clinch. It is a relatively safe thing to do, although no combat activity is without its dangers. There are two kinds of wrestling drills that will give you the opportunity to develop your skills for this phase of the fight. The first treats the initial part of the clinch where you are trying to throw and to block throws. The second deals with transitioning from throwing to ground work.

UPRIGHT WRESTLING DRILL

This drill corresponds to the *randori* training of judo, which is entirely upright with little follow-up on the ground. The reason for this kind of training in spite of the importance of establishing a strong dominance on the ground after a throw, even in judo competitions, is how much time is wasted on the ground rather than focused on standing techniques. According to an old judo maxim, throwing is seven times harder to get good at than ground work. In absolute terms this makes little sense as there can be just as much complexity in ground fighting or in free striking as in clinch work, but the maxim reflects that fact that winning or losing the clinch phase can happen so quickly that many fighters find it quite bewildering. It is very easy to lose your balance, slip, and suddenly end up underneath a highly trained athlete who is punching your lights out. Many mixed martial arts competitors who have trained for months or even years have lost embarrassingly quickly to a swift throw and finishing follow-up in the first round.

For this drill, beginning from a standing position several feet apart and quite outside each other's grasp, you and your partner are trying to take each other to the ground. How exactly you do this is up to you. Use all the throws. The objective is to make your training partner fall down either to his hands and knees, his hips, or his back. Going down to one or both knees and one hand and then getting back up is fine, but going to a full turtle position counts as a loss here. You can see the sense in this kind of training. In mixed martial arts going to turtle is as bad as or even worse than going to your back, so making your opponent fall down into either position is equally good. An interesting situation develops in this drill where your partner will go down to both knees, possibly as part of a double leg throw attempt, and you try to force him down farther into a turtling position while he tries to get back up without placing both hands on the ground at once. This translates into fighting in the MMA ring where if you do go down, you have to be ready to get up right away and even have one arm ready to defend yourself or counterattack with. Be quite ready to apply submissions or submission attempts, such as the guillotine choke, at any time. Consider occasionally adopting a double overhook grip and pulling your opponent forward into the ground. This gives you some preparation for setting up knees in the clinch. You will find yourselves developing some very interesting fighting tactics for handling the grappling aspects of the clinch with this drill.

TRANSITIONAL WRESTLING DRILL

Because it is crucial to be able to follow a throw with a position of dominance on the ground, a lot of time must be spent doing this wrestling drill as well. The difference between the transitional wrestling drill and the upright wrestling drill may seem subtle, but subtle things can make big differences in fight preparation. In the transitional wrestling drill, starting from a standing position, the objective is to establish a position of dominance on the ground for three seconds or more. The three-second number is somewhat arbitrary, so there is nothing wrong with making the magic number ten seconds or more. There are four positions you are aiming at achieving on the ground: top position in the guard, any pin, top position on the turtle, or back control with hooks in whether on top or on the bottom. You will find with these rules that you both spend a lot of time standing, but you also scuffle on the ground too. As in any fighting drill for MMA, a submission is a victory.

Striking in the Clinch

It is difficult to train for striking in the clinch due to how dangerous and powerful the strikes at close range can be. Kneeing someone in the face is quite devastating if done right. Unless you have an unlimited supply of training partners, you had better take care in how you prepare for this part of the fight. While being good at wrestling in the clinch is the foundation of clinch fighting, striking in the clinch makes it complete. With striking added, the gripping strategy changes somewhat. It is like walking through an enchanted portal and entering into a hidden new world of grappling.

Now a single overhook around the back of the head is a useful way to feed your opponent's face into your fist or elbow. A double overhook, seen as a position of weakness in wrestling relative to the double underhook, can suddenly become the most devastating grip you can wield as you use it to shoot powerful knees into your antagonist's face and head. Of course, the double overhook–knee combination can be defeated with a quick double underhook response, but only if you are fast enough to shoot your arms under your opponent's, pull in, and prevent yourself from getting bent over and kneed to oblivion. If both of you have double overhooks on each other, the one with his arms on the inside has the advantage. Therefore if you are in the weaker position, go for the double underhook or swim your arms inside for the dominant inside double overhook grip.

To strike effectively in the clinch, you have to withdraw the body part you are striking with swiftly and then quickly bring it back in to hit your opponent. This can be a very tricky thing to do against another trained opponent! This is why live drilling is needed, along with lots of practice and excellent judo or wrestling ability as a base for it all.

CLINCH STRIKING DRILL

This drill is an excellent way to develop your tactics and movements for striking in the clinch. It includes the same rules as the upright wrestling drill, but adds striking to them. However, you may only strike when you are gripping your partner with one or both hands. No free striking is allowed. If it were it would be too easy to get sidetracked from your objective by free striking too much. The typical grips for striking from the clinch are the single overhook grip for delivering punches and elbows to the face with the other hand and the double overhook grip for executing knees to the head. However, you will find other grips have their striking applications too. Kneeing to the body from various grips can have some effect, for instance. As always, it is very important not to hit each other hard in training. Do this drill at times with one partner going exclusively for throws and the other only trying to score hits. Another variety is to have both of you primarily trying for hits. The essential drill, however, is for both fighters to go for strikes and throws about equally.

Because this drill has to be controlled for safety reasons, it can never be fully realistic. To complement it, it is very important to strike the heavy bag and focus mitts in positions resembling those of the arena. The single overhook can be applied to a heavy bag as you pound away at the bag with your other arm. It is quite a different thing hitting the bag with one arm around it from having all the windup space you want while hitting it freely without a grip on it. Make sure you train both sides for this as with everything else. You can also practice your double overhook and your knee on the heavy bag. It does not resemble the actual position of delivery in the match as well as the single overhook does, though. In an actual match, you will have bent your opponent down toward your knee, whereas the heavy bag stays stiff and upright. However, it is a reasonable approximation. If you can hang the heavy bag horizontally from the ceiling with a chain at each end, this will be perfect for developing your skill at this move, one of the most effective in the mixed martial arts. You can get something out of practicing these techniques in the air too, as a kind of clinch shadowboxing.

With your coach or training partner, you need to get an actual grip on a real person in order to have a closer approximation to combat than the bag hitting can afford you. This is simple in concept, but must be done carefully so as not to hurt your partner. It can be done with focus mitts or a shield. Have your coach hold the solid pad in front of his face. Grab the back of his head for the single overhook grip and strike the pad. Practice this also for the double overhook knee. Have your partner hold a solid shield in front while you take the double overhook grip, bending him over, and bang away at the shield with knees. Practice dragging your partner around with the double overhook, and knee the shield from the left and right sides as you keep him off balanced by shifting the direction of your drag frequently.

The three forms of drill outlined here—fighting, hitting the bag, and striking focus pads—are all needed in about equal proportions to become good at striking in the clinch. It is not good enough to be able to set up a strike; you must be able to make it powerful—but not just powerful, rather it must be powerful at precisely the point of impact. Of course, in a match, the desired point of impact is always moving about. Therefore, developing tactical setup with the sparring drill, sheer force with the bag drill, and a combination of both with the focus pad drill are what is needed here. In a way you could look at these drills as the core components of a successful mixed martial arts match, not because they are the only ones you need, but because they address the most pivotal part of the match. They suddenly make your wrestling and judo gripping skills a whole lot more dangerous, as they bring standing wrestling to its combative perfection. They are also almost unique to mixed martial arts because they are banned for safety reasons from most other events. Muay Thai deserves the accolade for doing the most to nurture these awesome skills that fill the missing link between grappling and striking. They are defining features of MMA, on the surface appearing like barbaric brawling moves but in fact very difficult to master skills of primeval, ageless human combat.

Free Striking

What makes MMA so difficult as a sport is how many different kinds of skills you need to master. But just as we have noticed that because of the use of striking, grappling in MMA is a little bit more simplified than that of pure grappling events, so too striking becomes a little pared down from that of pure striking competitions. To sum up the effect of the blending of skills in mixed martial arts, you could say that it streamlines everything. The paradox is that because of the complexity of mixing the two sets of skills together each gets pared down to its most effective moves. The sophistication forces the refining.

Even in cases where free striking does not finish the match, it often plays a major role in wearing down the loser before the finishing moves. However, free striking does often end matches by knockout, technical knockout, referee stoppage, or inability to continue. But in MMA all skills—ground grappling, clinch wrestling, clinch striking, and free striking—are needed in about equal proportions. You might like to refer to them as the four wheels of the car or the four limbs of the MMA body. Your ability to finish off an opponent with a standing free strike may owe just as much to your ability to wrestle well and keep the fight upright as it owes to your striking abilities. It is sometimes easy to watch an awesome kickboxer tear through an opponent's defenses, landing a vast array of strikes, and shrug off takedown attempts as if they do not matter and actually believe that they really do not matter. But if you think about it, if one of those takedowns had actually worked, the fight might have ended up with some finishing moves on the ground, and the free striking phase of the match might seem less important overall as a result. This is why too much of any single phase of combat or even stylistic bias can interfere with your learning the science behind the art of MMA. More limited combat sports may appear to fully cover certain aspects of the mixed martial arts fight, but because of their rules, their competitors do not pursue the same kind of strategy as would fighters using the same moves in a mixed martial arts match.

An excellent example of this is Muay Thai, a time-tested and fantastically refined mixed martial arts form. Upright wrestling is a full part of it. Throws score points, and grip fighting is a critical part of the game as well. Competitors actually spend a lot of time wrestling on their feet as part of their daily training regimen, helping not only with their throwing skills but also with their control of the clinch for landing elbows, punches, and knees and for being able to follow up after a quick disengage with effective strikes that take advantage of their opponent's momentarily unbalanced state. However, the match must be restarted every time one fighter goes to the ground. This means that throws can never lead to a decisive end game on the ground. A throw does not lead to anything decisive in Muay Thai. The fight will be recommenced standing every time there is a throw, with both competitors free of each other's grips. This means that no matter how much you like to wrestle, the majority of points scored in a Muay Thai match will be strikes.

Only a masochist would concoct a Muay Thai strategy based on continuously charging in and throwing an opponent. All the effort would be for naught because you would have to start apart again every time, and while you charged in, you might get more points scored against you with strikes than you would score with your single throw. Therefore, in a Muay Thai match you will be faced with an opponent who is quite happy to use the clinch as part of a striking strategy rather than primarily as a means to take the fight to the ground. In MMA, if you get taken down to the ground, the referee does not separate you and your antagonist, but often allows the match to continue, and it may end on the ground. For this reason, fighting in Muay Thai will not prepare you fully for the earnestness of the throw attempts in a mixed martial arts match.

By the same token, the clinch in a Brazilian Jiu-Jitsu match is not like a mixed martial arts clinch. In Brazilian Jiu-Jitsu, throws are an integral part of the art for their important role as top positioning techniques, but they are scored lowly. Also, strikes are not allowed, so if you end up being thrown or otherwise end up on the bottom, you do not have to worry about the opponent in your guard punching you out. You might actually find it advantageous to fight from the bottom position if you were to score a sweep and end up mounting your opponent, or if your guard skills are so good relative to your opponent's passing skills that you keep the entire remainder of the match on the ground and rack up advantage points for submission attempts from the bottom, or do in fact win with a submission from there. So, even though the clinch is a part of the sport of BJJ, training with BJJ rules in mind will not prepare you optimally for the kind of takedowns and defenses against takedowns you will need to fight within the MMA arena. However, because BJJ takedowns are intended to lead to finishing moves on the ground, you will notice that the throwing skills that Brazilian Jiu-Jitsu fighting develops in its athletes are stronger than those of Muay Thai athletes. The reason for this is the relative importance of throwing in the two sports, a facet of the points systems and rules. The same throws are legal in both sports, but in one sport they are just for points and in the other for taking an advantageous position that might last the rest of the match and be the beginning of the end.

Combat sports like wrestling and judo that emphasize throwing from the clinch and staying on top on the ground prepare their athletes superbly for these critical MMA skills, but they do not provide training in striking, either standing or ground, and do not allow for optimal development on the ground. Wrestling matches are over when one fighter's back clearly touches the ground, and judo rules consider a strong guard to be a no-progress situation so both fighters are stood up again rather than leaving the two to cope with the situation they have found themselves in. But the emphasis on throwing from the clinch that these rules systems insist on allows for the kind of takedown attack and defense that is needed as a base for both kickboxing and ground grappling in MMA. Therefore, a basic requirement of using strikes in MMA is not just that you dedicate yourself to mastering the art of hitting a fighting opponent, but equally that you devote yourself to the science of wrestling. Only when you are truly sure-footed, in the wrestling sense of the phrase, can you expect to win matches in the standing, free striking phase of the fight.

Boxing

By far the two most used, and most useful, striking weapons in mixed martial arts are your fists. They have the longest and most variable range of any part of you except for your shins and feet, but unlike your shins and feet your fists do not take one of your supports off the ground every time you strike with them. Boxing is essential for every mixed martial artist. Boxing is a noble art in itself, and very ancient. You need to think of it this way rather than as merely a part of your complete repertoire. Boxing is so important to MMA that it is the fists that are protected, and no other part of the body except the groin, in most professional bouts. You should train for boxing on your feet, but keep in mind that your upright boxing skills will be transferable to a large degree to striking in the clinch and on the ground.

It would seem almost pedantic to enumerate here all the training methods of boxing. The sport is so universally known and understood that we need not be overly detailed here in our description of it. To be sure, you need your coach to have you hit the focus mitts and pads a great deal at full speed and force. This kind of training develops your ability to hit at all different angles in the heat of a match. Your coach will move the mitts and pads around and will walk around the ring too, getting you to practice the kind of footwork you will need in a real MMA fight. Being able to spring back and forward in order to evade a strike but then riposte at full power can be learned with the pads and focus mitts, as can circular stepping and frankly every kind of stepping and springing there is.

Better than mechanical fitness-like drills, which are of course good for you too, the live drill of moving around hitting focus pads and mitts makes you learn real combat stepping and accurate, full-power hitting. You will find that most of the time you should not cross your feet over in front of each other while stepping. Rather than walking as you would normally, you push one foot forward and then the other one trails it, rather than crossing in front of it. The most important reason for this is that it is a more exact way to shift position than to take strides. You can change your position by small increments and stay in a ready-to-fight stance by not crossing your feet. You will find yourself doing it naturally in this drill in order to keep yourself ready to hit the targets at all times. By making your hitting drills alive rather than dead, by moving around with a real person and striking with full speed and power at targets very close to the real targets you would hit in a fight, you learn to step and hit just as you would in the cage.

Bag training is important too because you cannot always have your coach actively move around for you, but focus mitt and pad training is superior because it more accurately approximates fighting in the ring and is done with no less power. It is one thing to hit a bag hanging from a hook and another thing to hit another human being moving around the ring. A bag swinging back at you and an opponent swinging back at you are altogether different experiences! Your coach should at times throw some gentle punches with the focus mitts to remind you of your duty to defend yourself and keep yourself guarded. Your coach may also wear a head guard and torso guard in order to allow you to strike the actual targets too. However, do not spar with the focus mitts or pads; use this kind of training primarily for developing your offense. Sparring is its own thing.

For sparring you have the option to either wear head protection or not, but it is recommended that you divide your sessions to accommodate both. When sparring with headgear you can go at it hard as in a real match, but your head size is unrealistically huge. Without it you need to take care not to hit each other hard, so it is unrealistic in this aspect, but at least your head is the same size it will be in a competition.

Boxing defense involves a lot of pivoting, twisting, bobbing, weaving, and swaying at the hips and knees. Taking punches on the shoulder and then retaliating with a big punch from the other side is something you really learn only from sparring, as is the art of avoiding the point of maximum impact of an attacker's punch by a mere fraction of an inch and thereby saving yourself energy and time for your response. These defenses are good to learn. By taking your opponent's target slightly out of his effective range and then quickly responding with your own attack, you are using very effective tactics for fighting a real opponent who does not have a grip on you or has a weak grip on you. When an opponent has committed to an attack, he is most vulnerable to swift counterattack. Boxing provides excellent training for this. If you do not isolate boxing as its own combative activity within your training regimen, you will find yourself relying too heavily on wrestling when up close to your opponent, and you will not develop the kind of striking skills you need with your hands. It is, after all, quite possible to strike an opponent very effectively without gripping him. If your striking training is always mixed with gripping, you will not learn how to strike free of grips.

So, to drill boxing for your mixed martial arts training, you ought to do boxing as boxing, which forces you to keep striking and to dodge the opponent's strikes. It is a focused and intense study of hitting with the fists, something you need very much. You need to be able to hit your opponent before you clinch and immediately upon disengaging. Boxing helps you perfect these two skills. Hitting while in the clinch is developed in its own drills outlined in this chapter and is really more of an extension of wrestling than of boxing because of how much the gripping changes the nature of your interaction with your opponent. One thing to understand about boxing's relationship to MMA, however, is that ducking down low to evade attacks and to set up uppercuts and so on is rather dangerous in mixed martial arts because you could get kneed in the face or struck on the back of the head. So you ought to consciously not make much use of this tactic in your drills. A good weight for boxing gloves is sixteen ounces, so that the gloves are soft enough to allow you to go at it relatively hard, and you can thereby develop quite realistic movements without worrying too much about harming your training partners. Caution is always necessary, however.

DIRTY BOXING DRILL

All boxers know what the "dirty" moves are. These are the techniques that are considered impure from the point of view of the noble art. However, from the perspective of the MMA fighter, these techniques are quite helpful. In fact, these moves have already been covered in the clinch striking drill outlined earlier, but you will remember that they were only to be used once a grip has been taken, and they are mixed in with throwing techniques.

Dirty Cross

In the dirty boxing drill, gripping behind the head to set up strikes with the other hand, elbowing, and hammer striking the back of the head are all to be used in addition to the pure boxing punches. The point of the drill is to box and dirty box with each other and not to throw each other. You are trying to develop skill at getting in some of the clinch strikes as part of your entire boxing strategy. You will learn to use free strikes to lead into a clinch strike and then, as your opponent is trying to respond to your grip, to quickly release your hold in order to retract and then swing your body into a powerful free strike. While you should both not try to throw each other, pushing and jostling to facilitate your dirty striking are of course part and parcel of this drill.

RETRACTING PUNCH

In a clinch with your adversary, push off him with your forward arm and retract your back arm and your whole upper body. How much you do so depends on the exact position you are in at the time. You might even step backward.

Then, making use of the windup space you have suddenly opened up for yourself, you deliver a powerful cross punch or elbow into your antagonist's face.

You can develop the movements for this technique on the heavy bag by pushing off it with your lead hand or forearm, leaning back, or leaning and stepping back together and then punching as hard as you can with your back fist at what would be your opponent's face range.

Retracting Punch Push Off
Adam (on right) pushes himself back away from Chris with his left arm, generating space for the punch.

Retracting Punch
Adam uses the newly made space to deliver a very powerful right cross to Chris's face.

Kicking and Kneeing

While the clinching knee attack to the face stands alone as the best leg strike in mixed martial arts, the most useful of all the free kicks is the back leg roundhouse kick. It is possible to kick very powerfully to the thigh, ribs, and even head with it, and it can be delivered with a jump. The free knee strike is also useful, particularly as a jumping attack to the head; however, a setup step may be necessary to develop the height needed for it to work. Either of these techniques to the head can quite easily score a knockout, so they are well worth training for. They are both techniques to use when your opponent is not fully pre-pared to defend himself, either as surprise moves or for adding a nice finishing touch to an adversary who is already tired and disoriented.

By comparison, the other kicks are not so important in MMA. Any kind of kick with the front leg is not very powerful relative to the energy cost in executing it, and it invites get-ting grabbed by your opponent. The spinning back kick is very powerful, but it involves twisting yourself around precariously, so it cannot be a mainstay of your attacking strategy. It is rather something to use when you think your adversary is in a defen-sive mode and is not expecting an attack from that angle.

As the most important part of your kicking arsenal, you must train to execute your back leg roundhouse kicks and knee attacks with either leg. Train yourself to kick with your back leg from both your normal fighting stance and from the opposite side in front stance. If you deliver the same roundhouse kick with the same leg all the time, this is only half as effective as being able to switch in the heat of the action into your opposite side in front stance and score an unexpected kick with your other leg's shin. You really need to be ambidextrous to be the best you can be in MMA.

The powerful movement of the roundhouse kick is wit-nessed in soccer, where this leg strike is used to good effect. Of course in soccer the top of the foot is used rather than the shin, but it is still the same kick: an angular twisting kick. To gently pass the ball to another player or to dribble it, a foot sweep–like motion is used. Sometimes a push kick is performed to stop the ball or to jab it out a short distance to another player. But to kick the ball a long way, or to propel it very hard and fast, the roundhouse kick is employed, kicking the ball with the top of the ankle while rotating the body. While kicking a ball is not quite the same thing as kicking a person, there is something to be said for soccer, with all its running, stopping and starting, leaping, and kicking, as a form of occasional cross training for mixed martial arts. And the choice of the roundhouse kick in soccer to propel the ball the farthest helps to demonstrate the superiority of this kick over all the others.

The same kind of training applies to kicking as it does for punching. Having your coach hold kicking pads and shields for you at various levels while moving about the ring is very important, for the same reasons as for boxing. Weakening the opponent's thigh is a particularly sensible tactic for using the roundhouse kick. A tired thigh slows the whole body down. Thighs are important muscles for grappling, too, so wearing down your opponent's front thigh is a big help generally. It is rather easy to hit an opponent's thigh with your shin because there is no great danger to you in doing so. Your opponent's response can be to block with his own shin or to move forward or back out of range of your shin. The thigh area is not within convenient range of the arm for gripping, although you should never be oblivious to the possibility of having your leg grabbed. The strategy to using a roundhouse kick is to be able to do it very fast and very powerfully. If you are good at it, you can score well with it because it is relatively hard to defend against.

To develop your ability to use this move, you need to strengthen your shins. This can be done by kicking the heavy bag and focus pads, jumping and running, and making sure you have a good amount of calcium in your diet. Because blocking this move also involves one or the other shin, one way or the other tough shins are needed. Tough shins are not the same as simply numb shins. You need to know your shin will not snap in two in a fight. Countless repetitions over months and years against fairly hard targets will help. Start easy and gradually go harder over time. Speed is also very important, since it increases power and reduces the chance your opponent can react to your kick in time to thwart it. To develop speed, practice repeatedly kicking very rapidly against a rather soft target. For toughness, harder targets are needed. Your shins are not just weapons to learn how to wield; they are weapons to be forged.

A good drill to develop skill in using your legs to kick is for both you and a partner, wearing shin pads, to throw kicks at each other and to block and evade as necessary. You can use your arms to block and catch your opponent's legs but not to strike with. If you do trap up a leg, feel free to attempt a throw, but do not allow this drill to become a wrestling match; the purpose of it is to get good at using your legs for kicks and to learn how to defend against kicks. This drill has a lot in common with the Korean combat sports of tae kwon do and taekkyon, both of which restrict hand attacks but allow the arms to be used fully for defense. Be sure to include some push kicks, knees, and spinning and even flying attacks. Just remember to be careful not to hurt your partner. Training partners are precious and need to be treated with care. If you do not have training partners you cannot train effectively.

If you are not as good as your opponent at kicking, then you will want to narrow the range and attempt to box. If you are better at kicking than your antagonist, you will want to keep the gap wide and throw kicks. Therefore, it is a good idea to do mixed drills where one partner is only using boxing skills and the other is only using kicking skills. The boxer will have to learn how to press forward into range safely and strike home, and the kicker will be forced to keep the distance between them with push kicks and so on, while both are learning to defend each other's attacks.

Mixed Drills

These drills simulate situations in which two athletes with different strategies fight. For example, one fighter may want to bring the fight to the ground while the other one would rather keep it upright. To be a true expert at mixed martial arts, you should be happy to fight at any range and in any phase of combat. Be that as it may, however, no two fighters are equal at every stage of the fight. One might be stronger at kicking or at the clinch or grappling. Therefore, an important part of fighting strategy is to be able to take the fight to your favored range against your particular opponent at the time. You do not, for instance, want to trade kicks with a better kicker, punches with a better boxer, or grappling holds with a better submission wrestler. Also, you need to be able to prevent your adversary from taking you to his preferred phase or out of your chosen stage of combat. This is an extremely important part of mixed martial arts, and it is one that is not really seen to the same degree in any other kind of combat sport.

STRIKER VERSUS THROWER DRILL

The most commonly seen mismatch of strategies is that of an athlete wanting to throw and grapple on the ground with an opponent who only wants to free strike. To drill for this situation, wearing adequate protection, have one partner try to rush in and throw the other while the other responds with takedown defenses and retaliatory strikes. It is important for the striker to try to score several hits as his antagonist comes in, clinches, and backs out again. The striker in this drill should not particularly try to throw the thrower, but rather should try to prevent the takedown and score as many strikes as possible. The thrower has to shoot in quickly and throw and block or otherwise evade as many strikes as possible.

GRAPPLER VERSUS WRESTLER DRILL

Sometimes a fighter who prefers submission grappling on the ground can create a problem standing up for an opponent who prefers a wrestling-based strategy and wants to execute a throw and take top position on the ground to apply a beating. This dilemma occurs when the submission grappler somehow manages to jump on the wrestler's back, get his hooks in, and proceed to apply the rear naked choke in the air! This is without a doubt the most visually spectacular submission grappling position there is. The wrestler will not want to simply fall backward as this could potentially lead to the completion of the choke on the ground and the end of the match. The grappler, however, has no particular way to force the wrestler down onto the ground and will find it somewhat hard to cling on in the air for an extended period of time. The wrestler will struggle to prevent the choke from coming on, and the grappler will try to apply it.

For this drill, the grappler starts on the standing wrestler's back in rear naked choke position. The wrestler's goal is to separate fully from the grappler and remain standing, or to end up in top position on the ground. The partner taking the role of the grappler is to try to complete the choke or take top position on the ground. The wrestler will find that it is important to stop the choke coming on by getting his hands on the choker's choking forearm and pulling it off or at least creating some space to breathe. Then it might be possible to slide the grappler's body around to the side and to actually throw the grappler to the ground. This drill is a good way to develop stamina in both athletes. It is not an especially common position in MMA, although it certainly does come up. It is justified for use as a drill because of how strenuous a position it is for both athletes and therefore excellent for conditioning.

SPARRING

In the last chapter we studied the strategies and tactics for combining the individual techniques covered in the earlier skills chapters. We will now begin expanding these strategies and tactics, looking into three levels of fighting: isolated sparring, full sparring, and competition. Isolated sparring forces you to focus on particular phases of combat: ground grappling, clinch grappling, ground striking, boxing, and MMA kickboxing. Full sparring is the same as how you fight in a competition but with full protective training equipment. Competition itself has its own distinct problems.

The first level is isolated sparring, which is a step up from the drills. Isolated sparring focuses on one particular phase of combat. You cannot avoid doing isolated sparring if you want to get good at MMA. Full sparring is what you could call mixed martial arts sparring proper. This is the sparring that resembles the full game of MMA except for the fact that you do not hit too hard. It is more or less identical to most amateur mixed martial arts circuit rules. Of course, this is where the sport comes together, but if it is done to the detriment of isolated sparring, you will find yourself quickly becoming a "jack of all trades and master of none." It is easy to get into comfort zones in full sparring. Isolated sparring breaks your comfort zones by forcing you to fight in every phase of the match. Mixed martial arts is the most complex combat sport there is, and it is easy to miss a lot of important fighting details by just doing all-in sparring all the time. Also, as pointed out many times already, the fact that you will not be hitting your training partners full force means that full sparring cannot be completely realistic preparation for a match.

If you were able to do full sparring safely full force all the time, then it would be almost the only kind of training you would need. This is what Plato's point about realism in training is all about. If you could train for competitions exactly the way you fight in them, obviously this would be the ideal preparation. The big blocker stopping you from training with full-power MMA sparring all the time is safety, and it is a huge issue. Not only will you have no training partners and coaches if you injure them, but you yourself might be seriously harmed and your career cut short.

If we look at how chess players train, we also see them focusing their "sparring" on various phases of the match, such as on openings, the middle game, and the end game. As chess players do their forms of limited sparring, even though they face no chance of bodily injury (unless tempers flare and the pieces start flying), they provide mixed martial arts fighters with the perfect model to help understand why it is important to isolate stages of the game and fight within them, working for dominance at every phase of combat. To continue the analogy of chess, the openings of chess are like the free sparring of MMA before the clinch. The middle game of chess corresponds to the clinch in mixed martial arts, and the end game leading to checkmate is very much like the ground fight in concept.

Any full-power combat sport is useful as a form of isolated sparring or, you could say, "isolated competition" for developing your MMA abilities in a particular phase of combat. Thus, wrestling, tae kwon do, BJJ, judo, boxing, Muay Thai, full-contact karate, sumo, kurash, belt wrestling, you name it, will all benefit your training. Every limited combat sport covers some range of MMA, so there is no full-power combat sport that is detrimental to your mixed martial arts training. The only issue in using component combat sports to complement your MMA training is that of finding the most efficient use of your time and energy. However, there are so many variables, often depending on the quality of the available local practitioners of these sports, that it is impossible to make any overarching statements about which arts to choose over others.

If you choose to cross train, and many MMA athletes do, you will have to make your own decisions based on such things as your size, weight, body type, athleticism, etcetera, and what is available to you. If you have long arms, then do not neglect boxing. If your legs are long, then be sure to train kickboxing, Muay Thai, or similar. The stockier you are the more important wrestling and grappling are for you, since you cannot rely on reach to end the fight from a distance—you'll have to close the gap, throw, pin, pound, and often force a submission instead. Ultimately, you have to be good at everything. As for the kinds of isolated sparring that are the best, we can certainly provide you with this information. We will also point out for you the combat sports that most approximate these forms of needed isolated sparring so you can make your own educated decision on what kinds of cross training you will choose to do.

Never forget that there are many tremendous fighters who simply prefer more limited forms of combat athletics because of personal interest or safety reasons. You can acquire enormous amounts of knowledge from them that can contribute hugely to your game. For instance, a champion wrestler can teach you about keeping your feet, gripping strategies, and executing effective takedowns. A tae kwon do expert can teach you how to kick very fast and accurately with your feet. An accomplished amateur or professional boxer can teach you how to punch. Why would you not make use of experts in their chosen fields? Just because your mixed training might enable you to throw a boxer to the ground or punch out a wrestler does not mean that you can outthrow the wrestler and outpunch the boxer. Consult the experts in each and every phase of combat, and respect them for what they are and for what they can do for you. You will not be disappointed!

Having pointed out the problems with overemphasis on full sparring, it is also detrimental to sway too far in the opposite direction and give it insufficient time in your training. You have to learn how to link all the phases of combat with sets of skills that only make themselves apparent to you when you are forced to move from one phase of the fight to the next and then quite possibly back again. Openings in your opponent's defense will appear at these moments of transition if he or she is not trained in full sparring. Conversely, you will not be able to exploit them if you do not devote sufficient time yourself to full sparring.

Let us not forget how critically important striking pads and focus mitts are. Sparring and pad work have to go hand in hand. There is simply no replacement for hitting your coach's pads at full force while moving about as if in a real fight. In a way, pad and mitt work are more realistic than sparring because of the full power element. When your coach taps you back from time to time, this pad work really does qualify as sparring. You should wear the same gloves or the same weight gloves as you will in the cage so that you are getting maximum realism out of the training. Do not neglect pad and mitt work.

If you are planning to fight in amateur matches, make sure your full sparring is consistent with match rules. If the rules for instance do not allow knees, then while gearing up for a match, do not do knees in your full sparring. However, if you are thinking of moving beyond the amateur leagues, make sure your long-term training goals match up with what will be expected of you in a professional cage. You really ought to learn the full art of MMA, even if the rules of different amateur tournament circuits limit how much of that art you can use in the arena. Also, if your interest in MMA is primarily for self-defense, law enforcement, or military combat, you will have to take an alternate approach that best suits your circumstances. This goes somewhat beyond the sport-specific scope of this book, but one simple and obvious thing to do is to train while wearing clothing similar to what you will be wearing in the kind of real-life encounters you expect to deal with. There is, for instance, a highly developed art of fighting in jackets and pants, found in the world-renowned *gi* fighting systems of judo and Brazilian Jiu-Jitsu as well as countless other prominent jacket wrestling styles around the world such as sambo and kurash.

When you actually fight in a match, there is a whole other set of concerns you need to address. We will deal with those in their proper place later in this chapter.

Sparring Equipment

You have to consider two things when choosing sparring equipment: similarity to actual combat and comfort. If you want to make your training more realistic, you should dress as you would for a real match. The caveat here is if the equipment makes you feel uncomfortable to the point where it interferes with the effectiveness of your training. For example, wearing MMA gloves while doing boxing sparring can be a health risk and at the least quite annoying. MMA gloves are not meant to protect the recipient of your punches. Sixteen-ounce boxing gloves are to be preferred for sparring as they allow harder hits and minimize the damage caused by your punches. Head and even chest gear make sense as well, so you can hit full power with less risk to your bodies. With regard to grappling, it is a good idea to wear the kind of gloves you will in the ring so you get used to the way they affect your and your antagonist's grips. However, if you find that they cause skin irritations because of friction, scratching, chafing, or so on, you might decide to only grapple with them on sometimes and spend more of your time grappling without them.

More training is obviously better than less, and avoiding unnecessary irritations allows you to train more. Does wearing a cup bother you while grappling? Maybe you will want to grapple without it. What about your mouthpiece if you are not striking each other? You really should wear a mouthpiece for safety reasons, and for getting used to breathing through it in a match. However, being good at grappling is more important than becoming comfortable wearing the mouthpiece. But then again, you do not want any chipped or otherwise harmed teeth. Consult your coaches and physician on exactly what safety equipment to use and when. Safety is the most important thing in your training. We recommend wearing full protection: steel cup and mouthpiece for grappling and headgear, sixteen-ounce boxing gloves, shin pads, and a steel cup for striking and full-out MMA sparring. If you or your partners get hurt, you cannot train. In the arena, hurting your opponent and not getting hurt in return is what the game is all about. So let the games begin!

Isolated Sparring

There are five major forms of isolated sparring. While there are many fighting drills recommended in the previous chapter, sparring is different. Isolated sparring is meant to reproduce as accurately as possible the conditions of one particular phase of an MMA match: free striking, striking and throwing in the clinch, and striking, pinning, and submitting on the ground. This means that while you spar, you are supposed to fight freely, using the tactics, strategies, and skills you have learned previously and continue to work on. In sparring, however, creativity is a very important thing, as you have to adapt to your antagonist, plan extensively, trick him or her, and try out things to see if they will work when facing another highly empowered individual trying to win. This is where you develop your own fighting personality based on your own interests, mental and physical attributes, and goals.

The cornerstone of your attack and defense is your ability to stay on your feet if you choose to. You are a joke if you can get taken down at will or if you get hit with a few punches, lose your balance, and fall down. Keeping yourself well balanced and your antagonist badly balanced is a big part of what this sport is all about at all ranges of combat. Upright wrestling treats this most fundamental element of the game. While throws and grips in themselves are not finishing moves, they are the most important part of setting up many of the finishes encountered in mixed martial arts. The clinch wrestling skills are analogous to maneuvering your military about in war. Outmaneuvering your opponent is what war is all about. You have to outflank your opponent, equivalent to attaining a dominant grip like the double underhook or overhook in the clinch. You may have to withdraw quickly in order to appear somewhere else. This is the same as releasing one grip that you are not making headway with and suddenly taking another one. While not many outside the military profession look upon boots, wheels, tracks, wings, and helicopter blades as being particularly tough, the guns of war are utterly useless without them. Some of the most top-secret military research has involved things like more comfortable socks and boots for the infantry and faster wings and jets for the planes. Often speedier, lighter tanks are preferred more than better-armored, slower ones. There is no military capability without maneuvering, and no MMA without gripping and shifting position. The highly esteemed Roman emperor Marcus Aurelius, considered to have been one of Rome's very best rulers, and whose book of life lessons, *Meditations*, President Bill Clinton read nightly, wrote that the most similar sport to military tactics is wrestling because of all of its encircling and positioning maneuvers.

Ground grappling covers the very important positioning elements of the ground fight phase of combat. While upright wrestling more than adequately covers the initial throwing and scrambling for top position on the ground, it does not allow for the maintenance of top position, passing the guard, and the other critical issues of fighting it out on the floor. However, clinch wrestling is such an important phase of combat that it needs its focus. Ground grappling needs its own separate focus so you can become an expert at both instead of working on them in an unbalanced and uneven way. Ground grappling for MMA very closely resembles Brazilian Jiu-Jitsu, and you could simply refer to it by this name if you wish to. The major difference is only that BJJ has a very precisely defined system of points for fairness' sake, whereas in MMA training generally keeping top position is adequate for proving sparring dominance.

Ground striking is the adding of strikes onto the ground while grappling sparring. So not only are you trying to keep top position and get submissions, but you are also trading strikes.

You will notice that in this kind of sparring, pins become quite devastating, as you have already noticed doing the drills suggested in the previous chapter. Things are quite different actually from the pure ground grappling, but the positioning skills you develop in grappling training are still wholly at the base of ground striking.

Boxing is an extremely ancient and developed art. Only wrestling can claim a more aged pedigree. Boxing allows you to focus on your most often used striking weapons: your fists. It also trains you to block strikes in very deft and agile ways, involving subtle dodges and shifts in body position, sometimes even looking like you are being hit, but actually only being touched because you withdrew yourself from the point of maximum impact. For mixed martial arts, "dirty" boxing is what is to be preferred. This means that you are allowed to mix in grips with your punches. So gripping behind the head with a single overhook can be a good setup for a "dirty" punch. You might even consider allowing elbow and shoulder strikes, but really, if you do this, why not allow the knees too; you are getting into the next kind of sparring. Boxing is meant to provide focus for your fists.

MMA kickboxing is all-in mixed martial arts sparring, but limited to the standing and clinch phases. It begins with free striking, progresses to clinch striking, and ends when there is a throw and a top position is established on the ground. In terms of allowed techniques, it is hardly different from Muay Thai sparring, but its strategy is different, as throws are looked at as ways to lead to a win rather than merely as moves to earn a few points. This kind of sparring allows development of the striking techniques, but with the threat of throwing ever present. It would be respectful of Thailand's ancient mixed martial arts heritage to refer to this sparring as Muay Thai, in spite of its actually being a little bit different from Muay Thai proper due to the inclusion of a small ground phase where you scramble for top position.

Wrestling and Grappling Sparring

While striking is on balance more deadly and direct than grappling, striking is almost utterly worthless in the MMA cage unless the fighter is also an expert wrestler and grappler. Punching, elbowing, kneeing, and kicking can wear your opponent down and even win the match, but not if you are thrown on your butt or in the process of having your head squeezed off with a strangle applied to your neck. You have to accept the fact that in a fight between a striker and a grappler, the grappler will win almost every time. But if the fighters are both good wrestlers, the better striker will win. This is a paradox, but a very true one. Striking effectively in MMA depends on good wrestling and grappling skills.

Wrestling has been the pet hobby of a great many world leaders. Abraham Lincoln, for instance was a famous wrestler, while Theodore Roosevelt and Vladimir Putin were both accomplished judo fighters. Sheikh Tahnoon bin Zayeed even invented a grappling sport, the famous Abu Dhabi grappling system. The full list is enormous.

It would not hurt to emphasize once again that grip strength is very important for any kind of grappling or wrestling. Obviously, grip strength is part of your overall arm strength, so lifting weights is highly encouraged. Practical grip strength for fighting is not an isolated strength but is linked with the movements of your entire body. For any kind of grip and pull back, dead lifts, rows, and shrugs are best. For lifting your opponent up, power cleans and squats are beneficial. Curls help in sinking in chokes and completing armbars. Body-weight lifting is also helpful. Pull-ups and climbing rope are excellent. If you had to choose only three of these to focus on most, then rows, cleans, and squats would be the ones to choose. Pulling back is the hardest part of grappling and wrestling. Therefore, your focus needs to be on the pulling muscles you need to pry free a limb for a joint lock and to sink in a choke. Next to this is fighting against gravity. To throw an adversary you need to get under your opponent and lift. So the pulling and lifting exercises are best, but there are no healthy weight lifting exercises that are actually bad for you. You do need to push in a match also, so all the presses are useful as well. If you find that you understand the strategies and tactics of grappling and can perform the skills well, but you are having a hard time of it while sparring, then quite probably you are simply too weak in the arms. No matter how good your gripping skills are, if you cannot keep a hold once you have taken it, you are useless. If your arms are weak, how can you expect to sink in that chokehold you trained so hard to perfect? Plato wrote that wrestling is more than anything the art of gripping and escaping from grips. Make sure you have strong hands!

UPRIGHT OR CLINCH WRESTLING

You may prefer to call this clinch wrestling because this name more visually describes the kind of sparring entailed. The object in it is primarily to throw your opponent to the mat and establish a top position there. So it is not so much the first person to hit the ground as much as who ends up on top on the ground that matters. For example, you might be the one who does the throw, but your antagonist might roll with it so strongly that he or she ends up on top of you on the ground. You could say that your throw was reversed. So it is important not just to throw but also to keep top position. Exactly what top position you attain does not really matter; they are almost all advantageous in MMA. Whether you force your adversary down on all fours and keep yourself on him or her in the *par terre* position, or you end up on top in your opponent's guard, or even better in some kind of side or mounted pin, you have accomplished a move of enormous tactical importance for the match. The exception to this is where you throw yourself into a back control and you get choked out. That would be quite embarrassing.

For this kind of sparring, holding the top position on the ground for a few seconds should be required. Let us say three seconds. If the bottom person can immediately get out and back up to his or her feet, then the throw would have done little more than score higher ratings for your MMA league's television program: something to put on the credits or repeat a hundred times in promotional material; it would have done little for your progressing the match if this were to happen in a real mixed martial arts fight. Ratings are important, but so is winning.

Also for this kind of sparring, be sure that you fully allow submissions. If a submission begins while standing and is finished on the ground, allow it the time it takes to be squeezed into perfection. So if there is an armlock, such as a flying armlock, begun standing up, then fight it out to its conclusion on the ground. If the attempter is shucked off and is then kept in a bottom position for the three-second quota, then he or she loses. If the armlock is completed, then of course he or she wins. One element to add to this when you are good at it is to attempt to drag your partner around with the double overhook grip, as preparation for use of the knee to the face technique in the clinch.

In addition to these ways of winning and losing, add that you can win by bending your opponent down with the double overhook grip and, keeping your adversary in this bent-over position, dragging him or her back, to the sides, or around for a certain number of steps. Only the kind of double overhook grip where both your arms are on the inside of both of your opponent's and where you keep your adversary's head down at about your belly range counts. The inside grip is dominant. If your antagonist has even one arm on the inside of yours, your knees would have much less chance of being effective. Dragging your adversary about for at least three steps is enough to display the kind of control you would need to launch knee strikes. After being dragged around for some time, your adversary will likely extricate himself or herself from your control and keep grappling. Just keep grappling, but score this inside double overhook bend-over like attaining a top position on the ground. This rule might seem unorthodox albeit interesting to a wrestler, but it should be kept in mind that many forms of wrestling around the world effectively penalize bending down at the waist for an extended period of time. Even well-known international wrestling styles like Greco-Roman wrestling and kurash, with their roots in battlefield training, limit bending low forward in their rules. Judo gives penalties for remaining in a bent-over posture. Their rules were devised with weaponry and war in mind. Old kurash texts point out how you cannot see the battlefield if you are bent over, and you can get stabbed easily. In MMA, you want to pull your opponent over, not to kill him or her, but rather to kindly and in all good faith give your adversary the gift of knees to the face. The rules of this kind of sparring for MMA are as follows:

- Throw your opponent and establish any top position on the ground for three seconds except for one when you are caught in a back control with hooks in.
- However, if a submission is being attempted, then allow it to be continued until it is either fully broken or it results in a tap out. When and if it is broken, the three-second top position rule comes into effect.
- Pull your adversary down and bent over with the double overhook grip and drag him about for at least three steps. Your double overhook grip must be to the inside of both of your opponent's arms in the dominant position for kneeing. His head should be at your belly level or somewhat below the whole time, the level that is easiest for your knees to hit at full force.

This kind of wrestling will train you for the kind of grappling on your feet that you will need for an MMA match. You go for and avoid throws, shift grips, and try to get your opponent in position for knee strikes and defend against the same. For cross-training purposes, judo and virtually any popular wrestling style, such as freestyle, Greco-Roman, folkstyle, and so on, have very similar rules to those suggested here. The people who fight in these sports are the throwing experts of the world and therefore good to learn from!

WRESTLING

The full game of wrestling is an excellent combat art in itself for the purposes of MMA. In wrestling, the object is to pin your opponent's back to the ground clearly, for an instant. Points are given for takedowns to a *par terre* control. There is about a 60–40 emphasis on standing throws and takedowns in wrestling. It is the most widely practiced fighting sport through time, the most ancient combat art there is, and it is extremely refined. There is an absolutely huge amount of knowledge from wrestling that is pillaged by MMA fighters for the purposes of their sport. It is highly recommended that you cross train in wrestling with wrestlers.

For your own specifically MMA-focused wrestling training, you should really include submissions. Wrestling allowed submissions until relatively recently in the history of the sport. It would be to your advantage to include submissions in your training, but otherwise play wrestling by its rules, which promote staying on top of your opponent, one of the most important things an MMA player needs to do in a match.

GRECO-ROMAN WRESTLING

Greco-Roman wrestling only allows grips on the torso, arms, neck, head, and upper body. Gripping the legs with your arms and tripping them with your legs are not allowed. Developed for battlefield use, this style is also excellent training for MMA, as it forces you to focus on dominating the clinch using grips only. Also, since bending down to grab the legs can invite getting kneed in the head sometimes, learning to grapple using only the upper body is very useful as it keeps you upright. If you intend to use dirty boxing and Muay Thai strikes in the clinch, then Greco-Roman wrestling is particularly for you as it trains you to control the clinch and master its gripping. Because you do not try to trip each other, you learn throwing skills that do not depend on putting your legs in awkward positions that could get your throw attempts reversed. In Greco-Roman wrestling, the fight of course continues on the ground, where you still cannot attack your opponent's legs with your arms or with your own legs. This too is excellent focus training for your MMA game, since keeping on top of your opponent with your body weight and striking is a major part of mixed martial arts fighting on the ground. Greco-Roman wrestling trains you to remain on top without relying on entwining the legs at all. As with any kind of wrestling or grappling that you do for MMA, always allow submissions as well. For Greco-Roman MMA-geared wrestling, you should of course only allow submission attempts involving the upper body against the upper body to keep everything consistent.

JUDO

Judo was created in 1882 as an integration of wrestling with Jiu-Jitsu. What judo can do for your mixed martial arts skills is similar to the benefits derived from wrestling. One nice thing about judo is that it allows submissions and requires long pins of twenty-five seconds on the ground. Further, judo does not count a pin unless you are entirely free of your opponent's legs, so you cannot be in any kind of guard or half guard to score. Passing guard, as we know, is a part of MMA fighting tactics, and judo forces you to do exactly this. In typical judo schools, half the time is spent fighting on the ground and the other half is spent doing upright wrestling. However, the *gi* is used in judo, making the gripping slightly different from no *gi* MMA. Judo fighters do not find this to be a particularly important difference, however, and many are also accomplished wrestlers.

There is a great deal of crossover among these three particularly popular international wrestling arts. Not only are techniques shared to a huge degree, but athletes move somewhat freely among them as well. In judo, the goals are as follows:

- To throw your opponent to his back with force and retain control of your adversary after you have thrown him
- To establish a pin entirely free of your opponent's legs for twenty-five seconds
- To obtain a submission through choke or armlock

GROUND GRAPPLING

Some of the worst things you could have happen to you are to be punched out, choked out, or locked out on the ground. Losing on the ground looks worse than losing with a knockout on your feet. Being beaten out on the ground exudes absolute dominance. The clinch phase does not usually conclude the match unless several knees are scored to the head. The clinch, if leading to the end, tends to yield first to a throw and then to a ground battle where the person beginning in the top position has a decided initial advantage.

This kind of sparring should begin exactly like the upright wrestling sparring. Both fighters should start the combat on their feet. From here they try to throw each other. The double overhook rule should not be applied in this form of primarily ground grappling sparring, since the ground phase is the focus here, not the clinch. Once the fight goes to the ground, it must continue there. The length of this kind of sparring can be undefined and can go on as long as you like until one of you achieves a tap out. Straight-out submission fighting is a legitimate form of this kind of sparring. However, because it is MMA and not a submission grappling contest you are preparing for, you have to focus on the ground positions that will most benefit you in a mixed martial arts cage. Therefore, you want to keep the top positions as much as possible and avoid being in the bottom positions. Submission attempts are of no consequence in and of themselves. If the submission fails, then "too bad"; you should not be able to rack up advantage points for poorly executed techniques. Defending against submissions while maintaining a top position is admirable in MMA because you are often in a position to retaliate with strikes from the top after shucking off a long-shot attempt to make you tap.

There really needs to be a creative balance in this kind of sparring among three things: maintaining a top position, improving your position to more dominant holds, and, of course, last but not least achieving the final submission. An easy way to score is to fight it out and simply be alert to who was in the top position or achieved back control with hooks in more than the other. If it seems that you were definitely on top for more of the match, then you win. If you were mostly on the bottom, then you lose. Of course, whoever gets the final submission, if one of you does, is the winner hands down. If you fight for a certain agreed upon time and then stop without a submission scored, then the winner is the one who was on top for more of the match. If you want to make this kind of sparring even more focused on the kinds of skills you will need in the ring, then make it the same duration as one round. Therefore, if the length of a round is five minutes, then you should time your ground sparring round to last exactly that much time. If there is no tap out in the five-minute round, and between two skilled grapplers there often is not, then award the victory to the fighter on top for most of the time. It can't be stressed enough how important it is to be on top in the MMA arena. While you can win from the bottom too, the advantage is with the top fighter, and in case the scrum does not result in a tap out, the advantage that the top person has in terms of striking must be taken into account.

BRAZILIAN JIU-JITSU

The rules of BJJ are tailored particularly for developing mixed martial arts grappling skills. They emphasize winning by submission, but balance this out with a points system that promotes top controls and pins. However, rather than scoring all positions of control the same, Brazilian Jiu-Jitsu ranks them by usefulness for MMA. There are also particular movements that score points on the ground, movements that progress your position from weaker to stronger. Passing guard gets you points, as does sweeping an opponent over who was in your guard. Also, the pins that score are those that you can most easily punch your opponent from. So the knee on belly gets points and the full mount gets even more points. Back control with hooks in gets you points, but please take careful note that if you do not have both hooks in, it gains you no points. Therefore, the turtle can be used as a defensive position as long as you do not let your adversary get both his hooks in on you. Many BJJ athletes find judo and wrestling to be helpful cross training, due to their strong turtle attack and defense skills and their throws. Dealing with the guard, however, is even more common than the turtle in BJJ.

The rules to Brazilian Jiu-Jitsu, created in the 1970s in Brazil by the Gracie Jiu-Jitsu Academy, spread around the world within twenty years of their inception, and the sport developed a wide following internationally. It is a rare example of a newly devised Western combat sport making it big on the world stage in the twentieth century. Its rules, which have a heavy emphasis on the ground stage of grappling, allow for the full range of wrestling and judo maneuvers, and in addition to these promote a high level of development in the areas of passing the guard, sweeps, and submissions. Conversely, although quite sensibly for what its focus is, BJJ rules do not particularly promote throwing skills, awarding few points for throws and prohibiting slamming the opponent to the ground. Regardless, throwing skills remain quite important for establishing top position on the ground. Other names given to this set of rules are grappling, submission grappling, and submission wrestling. The points are as follows:

- A throw: 2 points
- Passing the guard to any position of side control for three seconds: 3 points
- Sweeping your opponent in your full or half guard over and landing on top of him or her: 2 points
- The knee on belly pin for three seconds, with proper form: 2 points
- Full mount for three seconds: 4 points
- Back control with both hooks in for three seconds: 4 points
- An advantage is awarded for almost achieving a submission: 1 point

It should be noted that you cannot get points for a pin if you are in the process of defending against a legitimate submission attempt. You must first fully extricate yourself from the submission before you can collect your pinning points. It should also be emphasized that merely switching from one pin to another in order to score more points while on top of your adversary is seen as not worthy of awarding points if it appears that you are doing it only for points and not honestly trying to advance your position toward attaining a submission hold. Be these as they may, learning to play the game for points will not only make you a better player at this highly enjoyable grappling game, but will make you a better mixed martial artist, since the points promote getting good at the grappling techniques that are of enormous importance for MMA too.

The End Game: Scoring the Tap Out

Everything you have read and been taught about striking technique and strategy applies whether you are sparring or in a real match. If you are a striker, use the moves detailed in the previous chapters and further below to tire your opponent and put yourself in a position to score a win by knockout. If your match strength is on the mat and you are looking to win by submission, here are a few particularly effective combination moves that will help you get your win via tap out. We describe them here from one side only for ease of understanding, but they can be performed on both sides of the body, of course. Every submission is performed from a starting position. Thus the old judo proverb, *"Position before submission."* Be sure your starting position is strong and stable before entering, with lightning speed, into your submission move. Just as with striking techniques, use unexpected timing to catch your opponent off guard. Fake a different move in an opposite direction a few times, and then on the half beat switch into your choke or joint lock attempt. Refer to the basic versions of these moves in the skills chapters for detailed photos and instructions.

FROM STANDING

There are three good submissions available while you are both standing up. One is the guillotine choke, and another is the flying armbar. The flying choke is also a possibility. Do not be afraid to complete the submission on the ground if your antagonist falls down while you are effecting it.

Guillotine Choke

- Get your opponent's head under one of your armpits and squeeze the choke in.
- Thrust your hips forward and up to hang your opponent from your forearm.

Flying Armbar

- Grab hold of your opponent's right wrist with both of your hands.
- Jump up, wrapping your left leg into his throat and your right leg across his chest, pressing strongly against them.

- Pull back against the elbow joint while thrusting the hips forward to effect the submission.
- It is possible to complete this move while your opponent is still standing up, but if he falls down, simply complete it on the ground whether face up or face down; it should not matter.

Flying Choke

- Jump on your adversary's back to take back control.
- Apply the rear naked choke while you are piggybacked on him.

FROM TOP IN GUARD

Kneebar

- You are standing and your opponent is guarding.
- Grab his right ankle with both your hands.
- Step your right leg over his right leg so your back is turned to him.
- Pull his right knee into your groin.
- Squeeze your legs together to keep his leg tightly trapped.
- Press into his hips with your lower legs.
- Pull back with your arms against his knee joint while thrusting your hips forward.
- Fall to the ground to the right of his leg while you are doing this.
- If you can do the whole thing in one rapid, flowing motion, it has more chance of success.

Heel Hook

- Catch your opponent's left ankle under your right armpit with your right forearm and squeeze tightly.
- Place your lower legs over your adversary's left hip.
- Squeeze the leg tightly between yours and press down strongly with your legs on his belly and left hip area.
- Thrust your hips forward into the leg too.
- Switch your right arm position into the heel hook finish and effect the submission.

FROM TOP IN HALF GUARD

Americana Lock

- You are in your adversary's half guard, straddling your opponent's left thigh and pressing it down.
- Grab your opponent's right wrist with your right hand, with your right elbow on the ground to the right of your opponent's face.
- Snake your left arm under your antagonist's right triceps and take an overhand grip on your right wrist with it.
- Force his arm to the ground.
- While keeping pressure down on his thigh with your hips, crank his right arm clockwise with your arms, pressing your right hand down and lifting your left elbow up.
- Try to rotate his right arm so that his wrist is lower down on his body than his elbow joint. This puts extreme pressure on the elbow and shoulder and forces a submission.

FROM BOTTOM IN GUARD

Triangle Choke

- Use both your arms to trap your opponent's right arm into your chest or across your body.
- Hook your right knee crook over the back of your antagonist's neck.
- Hook your left knee crook over your right ankle and squeeze everything together tightly.
- While squeezing, place your adversary's right arm across your right rib cage, trapping his right arm under your right upper arm.
- Use both your hands to pull down on the back of your opponent's head while squeezing your legs in tightly. This will force the submission.
- If you are having trouble trapping the head down, particularly due to an opponent standing up in your guard, then turn your move into an armbar by throwing your left lower leg over your opponent's left side of the head, grasping his right wrist tightly in your hands, and thrusting your hips forward to complete the lock.

Armbar

- Use both your arms to trap your opponent's right arm into your chest or across your body, gripping at the wrist.
- Throw your left knee crook over the left side of his neck and lock your ankles together behind his back, pressing into it and keeping everything tight.
- Shift your hips so that your right hip is on the ground and your left hip is up.
- Pull back your arms, thrust forward your hips, and squeeze back with your legs to put pressure against your antagonist's elbow joint. This should force the submission.

Kimura

- Grab your opponent's right wrist with both your hands.
- Shift your hips out to the left and turn them so you are resting on your right hip.
- Keeping hold of his right wrist with your left hand, release your right hand.
- Snake your right hand over his triceps and under his wrist so that you grab your own left wrist with your right hand.
- Crank up and back with your hands and upper back while pressing down and inward against your opponent's triceps with your elbow and upper arm. This will get you the tap out.

Omoplata

- Start this move just as you would the Kimura.
- Grab your opponent's right wrist with both your hands.
- Shift your hips out to the left and turn them so you are resting on your right hip.
- Pull his right arm into your chest tightly while snaking your left leg over his right shoulder.
- Keep a tight hold on his right wrist with your right hand.
- Press your left thigh down onto his right triceps.

- Keep his right wrist snugly forced into your left hip bone with your right hand.
- At this point you should be sitting up.
- Press down on his back with your left ribs, triceps, and armpit.
- Lock your left ankle into the crook of your right knee.
- While pressing down firmly like this, push your hips forward and upward while pulling down and back with your legs.
- Since at this point you no longer need your right arm to keep his right wrist in place, you may release your arm and use it to help keep your opponent pinned down, for example, by grappling up his left shoulder or upper arm.
- You will likely already have achieved the tap out by this point.

FROM SCARF HOLD

Scarf Lock

- You are holding your opponent with a scarf hold from the left side of his body.
- Grab his left wrist with your right hand.
- Force his arm down so that the wrist is under your left ankle or shin and his upper arm is over your left thigh.
- You no longer need your right hand to hold his arm in place: your leg entirely does the work.
- Keeping a tight hold around his neck with your left arm, press your hips up. This cranks his arm around and forces the submission. It is the same kind of joint lock as the americana and Kimura locks.

Hand Triangle

- From the scarf hold, with your hips to the left of your opponent's torso, grab your opponent's left triceps by the elbow and press left and down so that his biceps is pushed into and across his face.
- Press your face down over his arm so that it keeps pressure on it and prevents the arm from getting away.
- Let go with your right hand and snake it behind his head.
- Link your hands together and squeeze everything in tightly.

- Shift your legs so that your left knee is being thrust into his back and your right leg is out straight.
- Press your whole upper body, using the force of your right leg and shoulder, into his neck through his upper arm.
- Squeeze your arms and face all together tightly. This should effect the choke. It works on the same principle as the leg triangle choke: the opponent is being choked with his own upper arm.

FROM SIDE MOUNT

Americana Lock

- You have a side mount with your legs to the left of your opponent's trunk.
- Straddle your opponent's left upper arm and press it down.
- Grab your opponent's right wrist with your right hand.
- Snake your left arm under your antagonist's right triceps and take an overhand grip on your right wrist with it.
- Force his arm to the ground, with your right elbow on the ground to the right of your opponent's face.
- While keeping pressure down on his left upper arm with your hips, crank his right arm clockwise with your arms, pressing your right hand down and lifting your left elbow up.
- Try to rotate his right arm so that his wrist is lower down on his body than his elbow joint. This puts extreme pressure on the elbow and shoulder and forces a submission.
- It is also possible to do this move with your opponent's right wrist trapped in your left hand and your right arm snaking under his right triceps and grappling your left wrist overhand. This time you crank his arm counterclockwise.
- Keep in mind that his arm need not be at 45 degrees or within 90 degrees for this move to work. The submission can be completed if the arm is nearly or even completely straight. In the case that it is perfectly straight, push down and forward with the hand holding his wrist and crank in and up with your other arm against his elbow joint.

- One last note is that you can effect this submission without trapping your opponent's left arm under your hips, only it is a little less stable.

FROM KNEE ON BELLY

Pull-In Armlock

- You have established a knee on belly hold from your opponent's left side where your left knee is pressing into his belly and your right leg stretched out straight.
- Your opponent is pushing on you or otherwise has placed his right hand near your chest or face.
- You trap his right arm by cupping both your hands behind the elbow joint and squeezing his wrist tightly into the left side of your neck between your face and shoulder.
- While keeping strong pressure on your antagonist's belly with your knee, pull into your body with your cupped hands and press in the opposite direction with your neck, face, and shoulder. This puts extreme pressure on your opponent's elbow joint and forces the tap out.
- This is the third most common joint lock in judo after the basic arm-bar and the americana. Without the *gi* it is a bit harder to get, but it is still effective.

Armbar. This most popular joint lock in every submission sport including submission grappling, BJJ, judo, sambo, and MMA can be done from knee on belly as it can be from a number of other positions both standing and ground.

- You have established a knee on belly hold from your opponent's left side where your left knee is pressing into his belly and your right leg stretched out straight.
- Grab his left wrist with both of your hands and pull upward so that his arm gets stretched out straight.
- Swing your right leg over top of his throat and fall down backward, pressing your hips up into his left elbow joint.

- Slide your left foot down his left side so the top of your left foot is pressing into his back.
- Pull back with your arms while pushing down with your right leg and pressing your hips upward into his elbow joint. This should effect the tap out.

FROM FULL MOUNT
Armbar
- You guessed it! You can do the armbar from full mount too!
- From full mount, grab your adversary's left wrist in both your hands.
- Pull it upward and into your upper chest so that it is quite trapped.
- Use your legs to pop your butt off your opponent's chest for an instant.
- While in the air, rotate your whole body counterclockwise, swinging your right leg over your opponent's throat.
- As you fall backward onto the ground to the left of your opponent, press your legs strongly down into your adversary.
- Stretch out his left arm as much as possible by strongly pulling back with your hands and upper back.
- Thrust your hips strongly forward and up. Make sure you do all these finishing movements at once, on your way down to the ground, and continue to do them once there.
- You should be able to effect the tap out even before your back hits the ground.

Americana Lock. This move seems a bit trickier to get from full mount than from side mount at first, but with enough practice you will find it to be equally effective.

- Grab your opponent's right wrist with your right hand.
- Snake your left arm under your antagonist's right triceps and take an overhand grip on your right wrist with it.
- Force his arm to the ground, with your right elbow on the ground to the right of your opponent's face.

- While keeping pressure down on his torso with your hips, crank his right arm clockwise with your arms, pressing your right hand down and lifting your left elbow up.
- Try to rotate his right arm so that his wrist is lower down on his body than his elbow joint. This puts extreme pressure on the elbow and shoulder and forces a submission.
- It is also possible to do this move with your opponent's right wrist trapped in your left hand, your right arm snaking under his right triceps and grappling your left wrist overhand. This time you crank his arm counterclockwise.

Keep in mind that your opponent's arm need not be at 45 degrees or even within 90 degrees for this move to work. The submission can be completed if the arm is nearly or even completely straight. In the case that it is perfectly straight, push down and forward with the hand holding his wrist and crank in and up with your other arm against his elbow joint. To help make this move work against a straight arm, slide your right knee over and place it on the ground tightly to the right of your opponent's throat, pressing down on the throat, shoulder, and face area with your right shin. Pull up against the elbow joint and press down against the wrist to make the tap out.

You will notice that the trickier aspect of getting this submission from full mount involves the fact that it is more difficult to rotate your upper body and arms into the finishing of the move. But have patience with this and practice assiduously.

FROM BACK MOUNT
Rear Naked Choke
- Start from the back mounted position, regardless of whether you are face up, face down, or sideways.
- Pull back with your heels hard into your adversary's inner thighs.
- Press forward strongly into his back with your hips, forcing his back to arch.
- Snake your right arm under his chin and into his throat.

- Grab your left biceps overhand with your right hand.
- Press down on his head with your left hand while squeezing your upper arms in together against his neck.
- Push your head forward onto his head and squeeze your right forearm into his throat.
- Make everything tight, and you will get the tap out.

Armbar. Guess what? You can do the armbar from back mount too!

- From back mount with hooks in, grapple your adversary's right upper arm by the shoulder strongly with both your hands and begin to pull his shoulder and upper arm toward your chest.
- While doing so, stand on your right foot.
- Release your left heel and hook your left knee crook into the right side of your opponent's neck.
- While you push back with both your legs, press your groin area firmly into his right elbow joint.
- At the same time, slide your hands down his arm so that they are both gripping at the wrist.
- Fall face down on the ground so that both you and your opponent are belly-down.
- As you fall, make sure your right knee crook and lower leg are pressing firmly against your opponent's chest.
- Squeeze your thighs together.
- Press both your legs backward into your opponent's body while pulling back and up with your arms and upper back. At the same time, thrust forward strongly with your hips against your opponent's elbow joint to complete the submission.

Striking Sparring

For all the striking sparring methods outlined in this book, you need to fully protect yourself. You need your mouth guard, headgear, steel cup, sixteen-ounce gloves, shin pads (except for boxing), and even belly protector if you like. Even then, you still need to be careful that you do not injure your training partners or get injured yourself. Ground striking, boxing, and MMA kickboxing are the three forms of limited MMA striking sparring.

YOUR SPARRING STANCE

One thing you might find when you begin to do striking sparring is that you discover yourself slow to react and have a hard time reaching your opponent in time to connect. You might feel frustrated with this because you can do all of the training moves perfectly well, can strike the pads quickly and powerfully, and do not have any trouble with wrestling or grappling. Then you begin striking sparring and feel slow and uncoordinated. If this is the case, the problem almost certainly lies with your stance.

The stance is what initiates all your striking movements. Believe it or not, every punch you throw starts in your toes and travels up your legs, through your hips, spine, and shoulders, and out your hand. It is a wave motion, like cracking a whip. The point of maximum energy travels all through your body frame and out of your fist into the target. Every strike is a kind of wave. If you crack a whip, what determines the force of the blow is the application of energy to its base end, and the energy then travels all along the length of the whip and out its tip. Therefore, your stance is what gives the whip its force. Thinking of your whole body as a whip, it is the balls of your feet that are your base, so in order to make your whole body lash out like a whip at your antagonist, you have to start the action violently in the balls of your feet. Unlike a whip, of course, the rest of your body's musculature can add its own energy to the wave, but the start of the wave is its most important stage, and if your feet are not springy enough in your stance, you will never be a fast striker.

Strengthening Your Stance. There is an ancient and time-tested exercise for developing a strong and springy stance. It is very simple. You adopt your fighting stance, with your arms in their on guard pose, and you jump up and down. If you like, you can throw punches in the air too, but the most critical element is the feet. If you are used to keeping your feet parallel and jumping up and down, you may be surprised at how different this feels and how quickly you will start to feel sore at first. Your forward knee, back ankle, and back foot arch might all feel a bit sore. Of course, be careful with them, but if you are patient with this exercise, within a few days it will feel very comfortable and natural to jump up and down keeping your fighting stance. It gives the kind of stance-specific strength, endurance, and power that you need both to last out the match on your feet and to generate powerful strikes.

GROUND STRIKING

As much fun as submission grappling is, you are dealing with more than just submission attempts and positioning on the ground. You have to handle punches, elbows, shoulder shrugs, knees, and sometimes even kicks! The form of sparring that allows you to focus on these things is ground striking. It is the same as grappling sparring in that you are both trying for submissions and attempting to establish and maintain a top position. However, you are also hitting each other. As always, when you hit each other you have to be reasonably careful not to harm one another. Therefore, this kind of sparring can never replace pure grappling on the ground, but it is an absolutely necessary complement.

Wear all your protective gear and your sixteen-ounce gloves. Start the fight standing, but only allow strikes when the ground phase starts. You know when it starts because your opponent will either be on his or her hands and knees in turtle or on his or her back in guard or a pin. Fight it out on the ground. Apply gentle knees to your opponent's head if he or she is wearing headgear. You will notice that a hand cannot effectively block a knee: it gets banged into the head, and both the hand and the head are hurt. Throw hammer fists and punches while in a wide and stable stance in your opponent's guard, keeping your posture mostly erect to avoid getting hit yourself, swept, or submitted and your knees flexed and springy. Gently elbow your opponent's head where you are able to. Hit an adversary who is in your guard if you can. Wrap in for a submission if it is viable. When absolute striking dominance is established, then you may want to declare it a victory and restart the combat. Absolute dominance is where you have mounted your adversary and have delivered a great many unblocked strikes to the face. This is the full art of MMA on the ground. Have fun with it!

BOXING

Much has already been made of boxing in the tactics and strategies chapter. Boxing is not only a drill, however. It is a distinguished and noble art all unto itself. For MMA training, do the kind of boxing referred to as "dirty" boxing. Specifically, add in upper body grips with your punches as much as you like, such as the single overhook. The fists are a legitimate striking zone to particularly focus on in sparring since they are the most used of all your hitting weapons. It might also be pointed out that many kinds of MMA competition may limit the extent to which you can use the other striking zones. Kneeing standing or on the ground might be prohibited. There might be restrictions on elbows. However, even when there are virtually no rules in a professional match, the fists are still the most used armaments of all striking tools.

To train boxing for MMA, suit up in all your training armor. Wear your headgear for sure! Put on your sixteen-ounce gloves. Wear your steel cup. Never forget your mouth guard. You might even put on chest and belly pads if you really want to go at it almost full force. Now, go out and fight like a gladiator! You are taking part in a several-thousand-year-old tradition of weaponless battle training. The fight with the fists was meant to be a relatively safe way to practice full power the fighting movements of sword and shield. Make the head your main target for your MMA boxing training, since it is both easier to hit than the body and more likely to lead to a knockout. Ancient athletes preferred the head too since their aim was the same as yours is. Whoever seems to hit the other person more in a given time period is the winner.

Because boxing is such an awesome conditioning exercise and so good for the reflexes, treat it like its own sport. Go at it for a few hours a day if you like, developing your stamina and skill. Another helpful way to train, particularly as you get closer to an upcoming match, is to go to it for the same number of rounds as you expect to have to handle in your MMA competitions. Make each round length the same as that of your mixed martial arts rounds. Therefore, if you expect to fight three rounds of five minutes each, do your boxing sparring just like this. Knowing how long a round is and the kind of effort you have to exert to win in this restricted time period is critical for winning. Allow yourself the same amount of rest time between rounds as you will have in your MMA fights. Since boxing has a lot to do with stamina and conditioning, just outlasting your opponent by being very defensive and then beating him or her up half an hour later when his or her arms get too tired to stay up just does not cut it for mixed martial arts preparation. You actually have to move and hit a lot in a given amount of time to make this kind of sparring useful. One famous boxer of ancient Rome simply kept his hands up in defense until his opponents could not handle the exhaustion and gave up. Some of his matches lasted a whole day! Imagine tapping out from something like this today! No professional MMA organization today would allow anything like this to happen, if it cares about ratings and profits. Modern people do not have the patience for this kind of thing, and it is reflected in modern rules.

Learn how to function the best you can in the time you have. Pacing yourself is always very important, but particularly so in events with timed rounds. Being too conservative is just as bad as being too liberal with your energy. Also, because of all the other elements involved in a full MMA match, you need to focus on your boxing as an offensive weapon particularly. Boxing will of course train you in all kinds of remarkable defensive skills, like rolling with punches and blocking with shoulders and turns, and will provide you with lots of evasive dodging skills to boot. Most important, however, is to develop your boxing skills so that you can win mixed martial arts matches with punches.

Winning is paramount. You win by making the other person lose, not so much by stopping yourself from losing. Train to win decisively. Try not to leave things up to the judges' decision. MMA organizations prefer spectacular knockouts and submissions anyway. Never forget your role as entertainer, especially when judges' points are up for grabs. We should add that everyone knows how spectacular boxing looks. That is why it always has been and will always remain an enormously popular spectator sport in spite of its limited nature relative to sports like MMA. Boxing limits the fighting to two particularly vicious and ultra-fast, lightning speed weapons. It confines the fighting to the fastest-paced elements. You cannot go wrong with boxing tactics in the MMA arena if you are looking to recruit fans or impress your organization's CEO.

MMA KICKBOXING

If you like, you could refer to MMA kickboxing sparring as simply "stand up," or even quite fairly and accurately call it Muay Thai. It is the striking counterpart to upright grappling. Therefore, you can still win by taking your opponent down to the ground and maintaining top position for three seconds, or by forcing a tap out through submission. However, the upright grappling rule about bending your opponent's head down with the inside double overhook grip no longer applies in the same way because this time you will be actually kneeing your opponent in the head, albeit gently, letting up only when absolute dominance is established by very many gentle knocks to the head. So, for this kind of sparring, start as far apart as you would in a real MMA match and begin to fight just as you would there. The only differences are that you will not pursue the fight for long on the ground, forcing you to get good at the standing portion, and you are wearing all your protective training gear including sixteen-ounce gloves. You must focus on getting in effective kicks, knees, punches, and elbows. If you feel you are being outpaced in the striking, you must try for a throw and establish top position on the ground. If you are dominating the striking, you should resist takedown attempts and continue to whittle down your antagonist standing.

The reason for training with this strategy in mind has a lot to do with ratings and pleasing the crowd in attendance. Quite frankly, the standing portion of the fight, provided it is full of kicks, punches, and so on, is more exciting and fast paced for the viewer than the more stationary and typically less action-packed ground fight. If you are an exciting fighter to watch, you might be asked back in spite of losing a match. If you are a boring fighter, even if you frequently win you might find yourself working your way out of a job. Sensible professional MMA organizations might even have a special monetary bonus for the most exciting fight or fighter at a given event. Two fighters locking up again and again in the same clinch or on the ground in the same position with few strikes is a disaster for ratings. So, to build up your professional career, devote a lot of time to MMA kickboxing sparring. Try to include spectacular moves where possible as part of this professional strategy. Therefore, aim to land flying knees, even at the belly level, flying punches, elbows, and kicks. You might even surprise yourself at how effective these techniques can be, now that you feel some pressure to make use of them!

Spinning techniques are also thrilling to watch and are in addition very powerful as well. Do not forget to try spinning backfists and spinning kicks. Often, regardless of whether or not these techniques even land, they are good for ratings because they look good. When going for throws, try to get good at big huge throws that launch your opponents, spinning them high in the air. Just think about it: according to many kinds of MMA rules, you could win by simply taking down your opponent with the double leg throw and then hugging your adversary tight in his or her guard until the referee restarts the match or the end of the round comes. You have shown more control by applying a throw and by staying on top, so you are the better fighter, but you are a terrible entertainer. Any strategic approach like this is bad for the sport of MMA and bad for your career.

However, if the audience ever gets the sense that an MMA organization is breeding fighters that are not really trying to win effectively, but are rather just trying to look flashy, they will lose interest in that organization's fights and it will likely go under. Mixed martial arts must always remain a real fight where two competitors are really trying to beat each other. Fans are not stupid. They can distinguish substance from style. We are not suggesting otherwise. We are simply pointing out that it is a fact of life in this world that spectacular is a good thing. If you can find a way to include flashy moves in your matches, it is good for you and for your employers. Flashy moves also show confidence on your part and can intimidate your opponent. Be real, and make flashiness a part of that reality!

FULL MMA
SPARRING AND
COMPETITION

6

In an ideal world, Plato would have loved to see MMA students and the soldiers in his republic fighting full out with full power every day. He probably quite rightly pointed out that approximating the real thing as closely as possible is the best way to prepare for real fighting. In his philosophically devised, rational world, the military would fight full out, divided into two armies launching stones and staves at one another while outmaneuvering each other through flanking, occupying defensible positions, cutting off ammunition and supply routes, and taking the war right to the other side's home city. At close range there would be full-contact stick and shield combat with special points awarded for hitting the most vulnerable areas. Plato felt that accepting a certain number of injuries from this kind of all-out, almost real battle training would be perfectly acceptable. The Romans and many others through the years have agreed and have used this kind of mock fighting as an important part of their military training. In today's world, fighting in teams with nonlethal ammunition and special protective gear is the modern counterpart of Plato's sticks and stones.

But even Plato recognized the need to focus on the individual skills that make up war fighting. Therefore, he instituted races of various distances in full armor carrying the weapons of war to provide focus on improving the speed at which his soldiers could maneuver. He also required that there be team fights with staff and shield, as small groups of soldiers often get isolated on the battlefield and have to work together as a small unit. Target practice remains important in his system of military preparation. For situations where weapons have been lost in the scrum, his theories suggest that he would have advised his soldiers to train in mixed martial arts and its major subcomponents, boxing and wrestling.

The purpose of bringing up Plato here is to show how even someone so focused on training real to fight real still divides that "real" into its component parts for special focus. It is the same with MMA. You cannot just train MMA. You must train all the phases of combat individually and put all of them back together again, over and over again. The separation is the "martial arts"; the putting them together again is the "mixed." This continuously repeating process of division and unification improves your skill and opens your eyes to new things. It is like kneading dough: you pack it up and roll it out, pack it up and roll it out again; eventually you make bread. Eventually you make yourself into an awesome MMA fighter. Mixed martial arts is the hardest combat sport there is because you have to be an expert at so many different kinds of skills. Isolate and combine; untie and unite!

To prove how effective isolating the phases of combat into their own sparring games is, notice how very little more has to be written about the specific techniques of full MMA sparring. They have all been covered in great detail already. However, some critical things must be pointed out that are particularly important for full sparring and are only fully apparent while doing it.

While sparring full out, definitely time your rounds to match or exceed the times you expect to fight in the real arena. Pacing yourself correctly is hugely important in MMA, and if you are going to go to all the effort of fighting full out, you may as well make it as realistic as possible. Also, as mentioned when we discussed equipment, be sure to fight in a replicated MMA cage or ring or in whatever can best approximate the stage where you will be performing. If you simply cannot acquire a proper practice arena like this, then lay tape down on your mats accurately outlining the dimensions of the real thing so at least you can get a feel for how big or small it is. This is not to say that you should falsify your movements to compensate for an imaginary chicken wire fence or ropes, but only for you to be aware of the size of the container and to generally try to stay within it. Using the fence and the ropes is important to your strategy. You can pin an opponent against the cage wall, and you can bounce someone off the ropes, yourself included. You can also get trapped against the fence or awkwardly rebounded against the ropes. There is a whole art to using the edges of the field to your advantage and to your opponent's disadvantage. This art can only be learned by training inside correct replicas.

Pacing the Match

Since you have used isolated sparring for working on different phases of combat, play your full sparring game as you would a real competition, without focusing on a special range of combat, or on anything else besides winning. Therefore, fight at the range at which you can achieve maximum dominance. Play to get to this range and keep it. If you are a better striker than your opponent, then keep the game at the free striking phase and shuck off any takedown attempts. If you can dominate in the clinch, then get to it and use it to try to set up devastating knees and other "dirty" strikes. If you are better on the ground than your opponent, then throw your antagonist down, land on top, and apply a beat down and possibly a submission on the floor. You could sum up the full art of MMA as one of essentially keeping the fight in your most dominant range against your opponent. The three major ranges are free striking, the clinch, and the ground. You can win in any of them. Victory through strikes can happen in all three of them. Submissions can actually happen in all three too because flying submissions can be done from the free striking phase and can happen in the clinch as well, even though they are most common on the ground.

If your opponent is an equal at every stage of the fight, then you are both better off keeping the fight in the free striking phase since you each might catch the other off guard with some quick and deadly strikes, and you will both stay relatively energetic. This is because any kind of grappling is much more tiring than free striking due to the added resistance of your opponent's full body strength and weight against you. But finding an exact match for your abilities is quite rare.

Realistically speaking, when opponents are well matched, the fight will tend to go to the one who tires more slowly. This must be given careful consideration: the fighter with weaker stamina will normally lose. So if you are fighting your equal in terms of skill, then do things to make him or her tire out faster than you. There is no exact way to do this, but it is important to point out that you will make him or her tire not through keeping yourself inactive and thereby conserving your energy, but by pressuring your adversary to become more active than you. Generally this is done by forcing your antagonist to respond with a flustered defense, so taking the initiative is to be preferred. It is actually more tiring to dodge punches than to initiate them, to defend against throws than to attempt them, to stop guard passes than to try them. When a fighter is reacting to something, he has to jerk his muscles with a sharper, more rapid motion than the initial attacking action, and this sudden jolting requires more energy than moving his muscles at his own will's beck and call.

Action is always easier and less tiring than reaction. As a result, initiating strikes, takedown attempts, and keeping top control on the ground all go toward making your opponent more tired than you. This is yet another paradox of mixed martial arts: you conserve energy by being more active, and you waste more energy by being passive. In a strange way, it is much easier to attack than to defend. If you can establish yourself as the initiator early in the match, then over time, you will become ever more and more dominant as your opponent gets tired of desperately responding to your attacks. It is like using the thin edge of the wedge to take the initiative in the match in the first round. As time goes by the wedge widens and at length finally splits your opponent in two.

This should not be interpreted to inspire fighters to launch a flustered over-the-top offense in the first round, or anything at all like that. Taking control of the initiative does not mean that you launch a hundred strikes and takedown attempts right away. If you make this kind of overblown attempt at taking control of the fight (even though it might actually work sometimes because your opponent is not ready for such an explosion of energy and you might catch him or her off guard), you will often just tire yourself out and sooner rather than later find yourself defeated. The reason that this sort of overdone initial attack backfires is not because there is something wrong with the theory of taking the initiative, however. All the same factors apply to the flurry as to the well-paced offense. The reason the overdone flurry often backfires is that you are not forcing your antagonist to react to your attacks. Rather, you are moving so fast and furiously that he or she cannot or simply chooses not to even try to launch an intelligent defense. Normally, your opponent will simply move around staying out of range, or he or she will cover up and take the shower of strikes on his or her arms and shoulders.

RHYTHMS AND TIMING

Think of it this way. If you had to hold your hat in your hand during a hailstorm and move it about to catch every individual chunk that was falling upon you, you would be exhausted beyond belief in a matter of seconds. If you simply placed the hat on your head and allowed it to shield you from the majority of the pounding ice pellets falling almost directly from above, you could outlast the storm's fury without tiring yourself even a little. So, in order to wear your antagonist out, you need to launch attacks at a pace at which he or she feels compelled to react to each one of them. This is the grand strategy of mixed martial arts, and of every other kind of combat sport too—really, of every kind of sport or competition in general. It applies to all ranges of fighting.

Once your opponent does in fact begin to tire from having to react more to your attacks than you have had to react to his or hers, you can start to throw in strikes or other offensive moves that are out of pace with the ones your opponent has grown accustomed to responding to. You launch, for instance, a first strike. Your opponent reacts defensively. You launch a second one, and your opponent starts to react to it too, expecting the third strike to come at the same interval of time. Now, out of time, like a half beat in music, as if your first strike was a quarter note and your second one an eighth note, your third strike is another eighth note and comes a half beat earlier than is expected. You thereby catch your antagonist out of pace and off guard. If you do not understand this description with words, then tap the rhythm out. If the rhythm is made up of three equal beats, then the third beat is very predictable. Tap it out—three beats of equal length. Pretty simple, huh? Now, make the second and third beats half the length of the first one. Repeat this rhythm over and over again a few times until you "feel" it. Of course, pause after the third beat. It is a set of three, not a perpetual motion clicking machine. Musicians would write it as a quarter note followed by two eighth notes and a half note rest. Long—short—short—longer rest: this is the first effective rhythm of fighting.

Miyamoto Musashi, the seventeenth-century Japanese duelist, writer, and teacher, wrote that fighting has all the same rhythms as music. This is what he was writing about. As someone who won more than sixty duels to the death, he was no pushover. His first kill was actually in a mixed martial arts duel without weapons at age thirteen. If he says that musical rhythms are one of the most important parts of fighting, then they are. You don't argue with someone as accomplished in fighting as he was—at least, if you know what's good for you.

Just as with everything else in mixed martial arts, there are no absolute rules as to what rhythms you should use in your attack initiatives. However, until you become an expert, you should plan your rhythms out and have a certain number of them ready at all times. If you wanted to be overly enthusiastic, you might take the time to write them out using musical notation, Morse code symbols, or something improvised. One way or the other, come up with several distinct attacking rhythms. The major tactic is to establish a slower rhythm and then change to a double speed rhythm without warning. You should have a selection of longer and shorter series of beats and pauses to select from in your match. One set might be in 4/4 time, another in 3/4 time—5/4 time would be interesting and unusual! One set might be as short as one bar, another as long as four or so bars. You can use rhythms drawn from your favorite songs for templates of beats to work with. If you remember a melody to match with the beat, you will find it easier to train with it and recall it in the heat of the match. Practice your rhythmic attacks on the bags, on the pads with your coach, and against your opponents in grappling, wrestling, striking, and full sparring.

Musicians would quite correctly argue that everything in life works according to rhythms, including of course the human brain. Your brain gets itself caught in rhythms, as does your opponent's. This is a function of the makeup of the brain, the extension and retraction of the limbs, the beating of the heart, and the bouncing of the body up and down as it rises up against gravity and then is pulled back down by it. You should really have at least five quite distinct rhythms of various lengths to attack with so in the duration of the match your opponent hopefully will not figure out what all of them are. This way you will not all of a sudden have to make up new rhythms and combinations on the spot. Because this is mixed martial arts, your rhythmic combination sets should combine several kinds of skills, for example kicks with punches, strikes with grips, guard passes with pins, and so on. Once you have fully absorbed the art of music into your fighting, you can constantly improvise new rhythms, change tempo at will, and become completely unpredictable. You will become like a virtuoso musician who can improvise anything to match the occasion. But even virtuoso musicians start by learning set pieces of music. To become a virtuoso mixed martial artist, you have to start with simple rhythms and then work your way through more and more complex ones until you can improvise at will.

Figuring out what your opponent's rhythm combinations are is also very important for fighting at a high level. Of course, none of this rhythm business matters much if the fight is unequal. If there is a quick takedown followed by a beat down, the word *beat* takes on a totally different meaning from that typically encountered in the musical profession. Nodding your head to the beat in a musical sense is quite different from nodding your head to the beat in a full mount sense. Rhythms are only useful for fighting if the two fighters are closely matched. This is why if you mentioned any of this information about music to a beginner, he or she might scoff at it. Mention it to a world-class athlete or coach, and he or she will likely even add to it and start a really interesting conversation with you! Initiating guard passes periodically are every bit as susceptible to rhythmic manipulation as are takedown combination attempts and series of strikes. Every combat sport and fighting art is based on music. Fencing, the fastest-paced sport in the world, fully depends on rhythmic strategies to win. Imagine your opponent getting used to your periodic jolts to pry open and bust through his or her guard. Then you attack at a half beat when he or she is momentarily untensed. You might very well break through. All good combat athletes are aware of breaking rhythm to catch their opponents off guard. "Float like a butterfly, sting like a bee," said Muhammad Ali. The butterfly's flight represents a gentle, leisurely pace. The sting of the bee is the abrupt breaking of that pace with a punch on the half, quarter, or eighth beat. Soldiers in war even get used to their enemies' rhythms of firing, taking cover, and reloading. Life and death have very often depended on identifying and manipulating rhythms on the battlefield.

To keep yourself from being caught off guard, you need to be able to quickly realize what rhythms your opponent is using, consciously or not, to attack you. The larger your opponent is, the slower his or her tempo is likely to be; the smaller the quicker. Clever opponents will trick you by varying their tempo. One way or the other, we each move to our own beat, to our own drummer. If you can quickly garner this knowledge of your opponent's rhythms, you might be able to predict when the next pause in his or her barrage is coming. If you are an accomplished and experienced fighter, you will figure out your opponent's rhythm in about the first fifteen to twenty seconds of the match. You must time your defense movements so that you are ready to hit back during this pause, starting your own rhythm. It is kind of a "dueling banjo" situation taken to the extreme. A good musical sense helps with this. Doing lots of sparring while being alert to tempos will develop this sense of rhythm in your mind. Most accomplished warriors feel an instinctive link between music and fighting. Their instincts are quite correct: the body must constantly alternate between being mobilized in full force for an attack and being relatively untensed, relaxed, and vulnerable to counterattack. If you can attack your opponent at the midpoint between two of his or her attacks, you will catch him or her not only totally unprepared for your assault, but at a moment of physical weakness.

Conversely, always keep yourself in a state of "alert relaxedness" so you are ready at all times to attack or defend as necessary. Being too relaxed makes you too slow to act or react, and being too alert keeps you too tense to act at full speed when needed. Being too relaxed is just as bad as being too tense— they both slow you down. This is yet another paradox of mixed martial arts.

Cross training in music is, laughingly, no joking matter. Athletes playing music at a good fighting pace and beating out their own rhythms on the bags or pads at the gym is a common thing to see. Many people train to the accompaniment of music and do not know why it is so helpful. Others know very well why it is so useful and take advantage of this knowledge. The key is to choose music with a tempo that follows a correct pace for fighting. If the beat (specifically beats per minute) is slow, you will train to fight too slowly. If it is too fast, your strikes will have no power because they do not have enough time to generate the wave power that strikes require, moving from toes to striking zone. The taller and heavier you are, the slower your choice of beat will be. The shorter and lighter you are, the faster paced your music will be. Use the beat of the music to provide a steady anchor for your own more complex rhythms. To train your mind to sense the rhythms of fighting, play music of an appropriate speed while sparring. There is an optimal rhythm for every one of your strikes in order to generate maximum power and speed. The use of music helps you notice this and memorize it. If you are a professional fighter looking for a hobby, then playing a musical instrument as part of an ensemble, where you have to adapt to the other players' rhythms, would be a very good choice. Of course, when you have fully internalized the art of rhythm, you will no longer need any external stimuli; you will be able to change beats, tempo, and rhythms at will while remaining fully in control of what you are doing. Music always matters, but eventually you will be the one playing the music and inventing the melodies.

Competition

Getting to the point of competing professionally involves many steps. Gearing up for the professional match itself has even more specific steps. We will describe how to build your career up to the professional level in a way that can broadly apply to anyone.

AMATEUR VERSUS PROFESSIONAL MMA

There will always be many more participants in amateur events than in professional events even if they attract much less publicity. Amateur mixed martial arts competitions were going on for dozens of years internationally before the Ultimate Fighting Championship and Pride brought professional MMA to everyone's television screen in the family room or den. Amateur events, since they do not give out prize money, are normally quite strict about safety precautions because the competitors want to enjoy themselves and test out their skills without having to recuperate for months afterward from a savage beating they had to pay for. However, amateur events will often have you fighting quite a number of matches in a single day, so conditioning is key. Because of safety rules, it is harder to score a knockout, so you often end up having to fight it out the entire match time. This means that you need exceptional cardiovascular stamina for amateur events and very quick, crisp, and clean strikes that the judges will notice. It is more than advisable that you start your mixed martial arts career on the amateur circuit before you move up to the professional leagues. While the strategy and even the techniques of fighting are a little different, amateur matches are the best preparation you can have for beginning a professional career.

This logic extends to participation in related combat sports. Wrestling, judo, Brazilian Jiu-Jitsu, grappling, Muay Thai, boxing, and other tournaments are all very tough, full-power contests, which are definitely good for getting you ready for the rigors of mixed martial arts competition. It is often true that professional MMA competitors are also highly accomplished in one or more other combat sports. These other sports allow for special focus on certain important aspects of the mixed martial arts fight. Wrestling and judo focus on the clinch, BJJ on the ground, kickboxing on striking, etcetera. These other sports are quite literally parts of MMA and well worth taking part in.

AMATEUR COMBAT

Before you can start a professional fighting career, you must already have a strong amateur one under your belt. Most amateur mixed martial arts tourney rules are limited for reasons of safety. You should not confine yourself to amateur MMA competitions, but you should also cross-fight in full-power combat sports. Particularly recommendable are wrestling and grappling tourneys, as wrestling and grappling are the base for mixed martial arts due to the importance of the clinch and the finality of the ground fight that often follows from it. Search out wrestling, judo, submission grappling, and Brazilian Jiu-Jitsu tournaments. Of course, this means learning to fight properly according to each sport's particular rules. If you do not understand and train for the rules, you are mostly wasting your time.

Striking competitions, providing they are full power, are also excellent. Boxing (Choose amateur with the head protection—it is not worth wearing out your body until you do real MMA!) and Muay Thai are particularly relevant to an MMA fighter for reasons already given, but there are other full-power striking events out there. Olympic-style tae kwon do is a very hard-hitting combat sport that forces you to use your feet, since the fists may only strike to the chest. There is nothing wrong with this limitation as long as you train hard at boxing and Muay Thai also. Focusing all your energies on the feet as you have to in tae kwon do will force you to get better at using them than you otherwise would. Kyokushin, Shotokan, and other karate styles often hold full-contact events, frequently bare-knuckled, where matches are won by knocking the opponent down with a strike. There are numerous kickboxing styles ready to accept new competitors. The point is that mixed martial arts really means "mixed," so mix it up a bit! You might even get some insight from doing a bit of fencing or kendo, etcetera. You will not be the first to do so. Of course, compete as often as possible in amateur mixed martial arts! That should go without saying!

Once you have started to get used to the pressures of preparing to compete and of competing itself, you will start to find yourself actually winning some of these local tournaments. Performing well in competitions does not only depend on being a good fighter. It also depends on handling your nerves, getting enough rest, remaining well hydrated, and zoning into the fighting spirit immediately before your match. You may find it helpful to listen to music and/or visualize yourself fighting to get into the "zone." All these skills can only come with experience fighting in competitions. There is no other way to learn them. To get sponsorship to travel to the larger national and international level events, you will normally need to show several first-place results. Any locally held international events you *must* compete in. Take advantage of them! You are lucky they are held nearby.

Just as we mentioned earlier how important rhythm is during the fight, it is just as important, albeit in a different way, in the lead-up to the fight. Getting used to what things to do at what times before a fight to get yourself in optimal physical and mental shape for the match is a matter of continual experience and reflection. Everyone is different physically and mentally, and you have to do some trial-and-error work regarding when to eat, sleep, exercise, what to think about, and so on, leading up to your competitions. Only experience getting ready for competitions can teach you these things. Your coach can help, but the art of preparing for fighting is so subtle that in the end only the athlete can really know exactly what to do. It is for this reason that some people who always beat you while sparring in the gym may end up getting totally destroyed by you on the day of a major competition. They are simply not as good at getting ready for it as you are.

There is also a whole other level of intensity to competitions that is due to the relative unfamiliarity of the situation and of the opponent in this more aggressive and serious mental state. Almost always you will be facing an opponent whom you do not train with and whose strong and weak points you do not know. This is why many athletes find it helpful to poke about for most of the first round to sense the opponent's rhythm, timing, and favorite moves. Then they think of the best ways to defeat their opponent's proclivities and in the second round go at it in more earnestness. This is not necessarily the best way to go about things. Really, you ought to set the pace of the match right at the beginning, with you as the initiator. Make your opponent play your game, not you his or hers. We have already discussed why this is so. It should not take you longer than the first quarter-minute or so of the fight to set the pace. If you are the one setting the pace, you do not need to worry so much about what pace your opponent will set for you. If you are the one leading the action, you do not have to be overly concerned with what your opponent would like to do. Your opponent does what you want him or her to do, not the other way around. This is the way it should be. If your opponent is also an expert at rhythms, then it becomes a musical battle. Start winning right at the start; does this not make sense? If you are both experts at manipulating rhythms, the fight will in the end go to the one with better stamina. Yet again we encounter just how critically important conditioning is to your career. A world champion who is out of shape is as vulnerable as a bug to a well-conditioned amateur.

WHAT TO THINK ABOUT IN THE CAGE

When you are in the cage, one way of reducing the psychological pressure is to take great pride in all the attention you are getting. Enjoy your time in the spotlight. Show off. Prove to the audience that it is worth their time to watch you. Really savor the experience. You are it. You are the show. In Muay Thai matches, the fighters bow to each side of the ring. They are paying their respects to the audience. One way or another, respect the spectators. Thank them for their interest in you.

A FINAL CHARGE

Take the battle to your antagonist and defeat him or her. Use everything you know. Listen carefully to your coach. Your coach's job is simply to remind you of things that you already know but are not thinking of in the heat of the moment. Remember that the purpose of the fight is to win it, not just to avoid getting submitted or knocked out. You have to out-perform your adversary, not just outlast him or her. You have to impress the judges. Ideally you can score a submission or knockout. In the ring, just fight and listen to your coach. Those are the two things you have to do. Winning is everything. Win. If you win you do not have to say, "I would have, I could have, I should have." It is much better to be able to say, "I came, I saw, I conquered." These words—in Latin, "Veni, vidi, vici"—are the only words Julius Caesar spoke after doubling the size of the Roman Empire, in spite of everyone expecting him to deliver a lengthy and bombastic speech. But you will not have to say anything. Your accomplishment will speak for itself. That is the way you want things to be.

After the fight, when you are interviewed, thank and pro-mote your sponsors, thank your opponent and the organization, smile, and begin to live the dream. Make sure you rest and recu-perate adequately after the match before your next one. Con-sult your coach and physician about this.

Appendix: Consultants

The following coaches and fighters were kind enough to discuss the vast subject of mixed martial arts with the authors prior to the writing of the book, sharing their experiences and providing sounding boards for ideas.

Carlos Newton, UFC Welterweight World Champion

Carlos "The Ronin" Newton has an extensive professional mixed martial arts career spanning more than a decade. As of 2007, his professional fight record was 13-13-0. From May to November 2001, he held the UFC welterweight world champion title. His personal fighting style, which he has styled "Dragonball Jiu-Jitsu," is a combination of judo, Jiu-Jitsu, and wrestling. His interest in the martial arts goes beyond professional fighting, extending to philosophy, history, literature, and psychology. He is a fluent speaker of Japanese and is able therefore to access classical martial arts works in their original tongue. Besides being a world champion fighter, he is also a dedicated medical student specializing in geriatric medicine. His notable professional MMA victories include wins over Tokimitsu Ishizawa, Renzo Gracie, Pete Spratt, Jose Landi-Jons, Pat Miletich, Johil de Oliveira, Yuhi Sano, Karl Schmidt, Daijiro Matsui, Kenji Kawaguchi, Bob Gilstrap, Kazuhiro Kusayanagi, and Erik Paulson.

Mark Bocek, Professional Mixed Martial Artist and BJJ Black Belt

Mark Bocek is one of Canada's first Brazilian Jiu-Jitsu black belts and has been studying the art for more than a decade. He first studied under Rickson and Renzo Gracie and then moved on to Nova Uniao, where he received his black belt through Joao Roque.

Mark is a fierce competitor and remains one of the most respected grapplers in the world. He has victories over Shawn Williams, Kurt Pellegrino, Jordan Damon, Mike Fowler, and Ryan Hall. He has also defeated Drew Fickett at the Abu Dhabi submission wrestling world championships and Doug Evans in the UFC. Mark is also 5-1-0 in mixed martial arts competition and still under contract with the UFC.

ACCOMPLISHMENTS

- Defeated Doug Evans by unanimous decision at UFC 79 Nemesis on December 29, 2007, in Las Vegas
- 2007 North American Grappling Championship advanced division absolute winner (Grapplers Quest)
- 2007 North American Grappling Championship advanced division under 170 pounds winner (Grapplers Quest)
- 2007 North East Grappling Challenge champion, 189 pounds advanced
- 2007 ADCC veteran, defeated Drew Fickett 8–0 in the first round
- Defeated Garett Davis in round 1 in King of the Cage: Capital Chaos on March 28, 2007
- Submitted John Mahlow in round 1 at King of the Cage: Freedom Fight 2007 on January 20, 2007
- 2006 ADCC North American Trials champion defeating Drew Puzon, Rob Kahn, Don Ortega, and Mike Fowler

- Defeated Kevin Manderson in round 1 by rear naked choke at Apex Fighting: A Night of Champions, October 14, 2006
- 2006 NAGA Ohio Championships 150–159 pounds no-*gi* advanced champion and the under 175 pounds black belt champion
- 2005 Grapplers Quest Southeast Grappling Championships no-*gi* pro silver medalist and 2005 Copa Atlantica Brazilian Jiu-Jitsu Championships black belt division silver medalist
- 2005 Bravado champion, advanced and absolute
- ADCC Canadian Trials champion in 2002 and 2004
- Professional MMA fight debut in 2004 at TKO 15, defeating Mark Colangelo by technical knockout
- 2003 Brasilia State champion (brown belt)
- 2002 Grapplers Quest U.S. national champion
- 2002 World Brazilian Jiu-Jitsu champion
- Three-time Pan American medalist in 1999, 2000, and 2002
- 2002 Campos Submission Wrestling champion (Brazil), closed the division with Leo Santos
- 2000 Hawaii State champion, blue belt division and open
- Five-time Canadian champion: 1997, 1998, 1999, 2000, and 2001
- Multiple-time Joslins champion
- 1999 NAGA champion, closed division with Joe D'arce and Shawn Williams (all training with Renzo Gracie at the time)

"WHAT MMA MEANS TO ME" BY MARK BOCEK

MMA is the truest and purest form of combat that a human being can test his skills and heart. MMA fighters are the most well-rounded and best-conditioned athletes in the world. Ever since I first witnessed the sport I was immediately hooked. I first saw the sport in 1994 and was amazed at what Royce Gracie was capable of; there are no teams, no one to blame but yourself. These elements really attracted me to the sport and made me deeply appreciate it, and I knew from that day on that was the reason I was born. Born to fight!

MMA is exploding like crazy, taking over boxing and everything in its path. People are starting to realize that the best fighters are in MMA; it is the realest combat sport there is and also much safer than boxing due to less head trauma. Nothing is more exciting than this sport; it will only get bigger and better.

Gary Turner, Professional Mixed Martial Artist

Gary "Smiler" Turner was born in 1970 in a small town just outside of London, England. His life became defined on his sixth birthday when he was taken to his first judo lesson and his martial sports life began. With dedication and determination taught to him by his father, he persevered for about four years until he finally achieved his first competition judo medal. After this the floodgates opened, and Turner would compete most weekends at regional, national, and international events, more often than not returning with a medal.

As Turner's career progressed he became county champion, competed for the British School's judo team, and after more than ten years of study achieved his first dan black belt grade. (Turner currently has three black belt grades and is second dan judo, second dan Jiu-Jitsu, and second degree kickboxing.)

At eighteen he started working the doors on nightclubs while studying at college during the day. Here he mixed with a couple of top points kickboxers, and he talked them into taking up judo and competing in an international event. In return, Turner took up Lau Gar kung fu and also started competing as a points kickboxer.

From here Turner's sporting career started to diversify. Points kickboxing led to light continuous kickboxing, and this saw him represent his second British team, as he competed as part of the WAKO British kickboxing team at his first European Championships and won the bronze medal. Turner would go on to compete for the WAKO British team at full-contact kickboxing throughout the 1990s, where he picked up a European silver medal before finally becoming European and World Full Contact Kickboxing champion.

Turner stopped competing at judo in 1991 to concentrate on his kickboxing. However, a chance call from the British Jiu-Jitsu team led to his third British team representation. His sport Jiu-Jitsu took place from 1994 through to 2003, seeing Turner compete on the ISJA, WCJJO, and IJJF sport Jiu-Jitsu world circuits and achieving Turner eleven individual and team world championship gold medals, amongst a smattering of other world and European medal positions.

Turner also competed during the 1990s as a professional sportsman, competing in full-contact kickboxing matches, achieving British titles for the WAKO and WKA and the European WAKO title. He also competed in the British Wushu Kwan championships, where he won gold to become British champion.

But Turner still found time for other challenges. In 1991 he became (arguably) Britain's first international mixed martial artist when he won the Golden Dragon Cup in Rimini in 1991, competing in shootfighting. In the late 1990s Turner also competed on the pioneering Lee Hasdell mixed martial arts shows, winning one fight by knockout and achieving a draw in his second event.

In 2000 a new challenge saw Turner start his K1 campaign. After a shaky start Turner had to develop his skills quickly, and 2003 saw Turner win his first K1 British Championships, repeated again in 2004. Turner found himself competing around the world in the K1 Spain (semifinalist), K1 Switzerland (semifinalist), and K1 Scandanavia (second place) tournaments.

Turner continues to pursue his striking career, mixing kickboxing with Thai boxing and K1 fights around the world. He beat Azem Maksutaj in Switzerland to pick up the WPKC world heavyweight Thai boxing title and defeated Carter Williams at the Arnold Classic in Ohio as notable highlights.

Recently Turner has felt a lack of opportunity coming from the K1 matchmakers and so has taken up other challenges. In 2006 he was due to fight Martin Lidberg (World and Olympic wrestling star) in Sweden in his first MMA match of his "new age." Unfortunately Lidberg dislocated his knee in his final training session, and therefore Turner wasn't able to compete. But he had started training for MMA, and when a proposal came to fight Bob Sapp at short notice, Turner leapt at the opportunity. Unfortunately Sapp decided not to fight in the last few days before the fight, leaving Turner fighting the MMA legend David "Tank" Abbott, whom he considered to be a much tougher opponent. Turner won by TKO in the first round and is now advancing his MMA career, whilst also making a return to the competition judo scene.

PROFESSIONAL FIGHT RECORD

- Kickboxing/K1/Thai: 25 wins, 8 losses, 3 draws, 13 wins by way of KO
- MMA: 10 wins, 0 losses, 1 draw, 5 wins by way of KO

Mark Simon, Mixed Martial Artist

Mark Simon has had a distinguished career in amateur MMA competition and coaching. He also served in the military, which informs his approach to the sport.

ACCOMPLISHMENTS

- Five-time Canadian lightweight Sport Jiu-Jitsu champion
- Two-time World Sport Jiu-Jitsu champion
- Undefeated in all matches sport Jiu-Jitsu 1998–2007

- Canadian Armed Forces 1992–1996
- Nationally certified coach, level 1
- Coaching MMA and submission grappling since 2002
- Multiple Canadian champions under his coaching
- Secondary school martial arts instructor

Adam Hensen, Mixed Martial Artist

Adam Henson began training martial arts in March of 2006 at the Hamilton School of Martial Arts as a means to get in shape and better himself as a person. He also loved the sport of mixed martial arts and thought that he would like to train in many disciplines to be a good all-round fighter. He began training in kickboxing for striking, judo for the clinch, and Jiu-Jitsu for grappling under multiple coaches, but mostly under Mickey Dimic and Mark Simon. Adam entered his first grappling tournament in April of 2006, winning first place. After strong success in many grappling tournaments, he started to train in boxing under Charles Biggs to improve his striking and get more ring experience. His first boxing match under Charles ended with Adam as the victor by TKO in the third round. After many tryouts and qualifying tournaments for the Canadian Jiu-Jitsu team, he secured himself a spot in the light heavyweight division (165–179 pounds). In September of 2007 Team Canada traveled to Jersey, Channel Islands, to compete in the World Jiu-Jitsu Championships, a major international amateur MMA event held once every three years. Team Canada brought home a silver medal collectively, and Adam brought home an individual gold—a great accomplishment considering that he had only been training for about a year and a half. Upon returning, coaches Mickey Dimic and Mark Simon arranged for Adam to meet Kru Adam Higson, a renowned Muay Thai instructor and professional fighter. They thought that it would be in Adam's best interest to train with him at the Phoenix Fight Club to give Adam a different perspective. Now under Kru Adam Higson, he trains Muay Thai, but more specifically, "Dutch style Thai-boxing." Adam continues to evolve into the fighter that he wants to be with the help of many coaches at both the Hamilton School of Martial Arts and the Phoenix Fight Club. Adam credits the professionalism and dedication of his coaches for his success. In addition to providing helpful advice from an accomplished fighter's perspective Adam generously volunteered to appear in the pictures for this publication.

Greg Woodcroft, Wrestler

Greg Woodcroft, a world-class wrestler, kinesiologist, and coach, has been an invaluable resource for the science of wrestling and how to apply this ancient combat sport to the mixed martial arts cage.

ACCOMPLISHMENTS

- Four-time OUAA champion at both 52 kg and 57 kg
- Three-time CIAU champion at both 52 kg and 57 kg
- Won OFSAA wrestling four years in a row at 41, 44, 47.5, and 51 kg weight classes
- Won many youth age national championships: two cadet (14–15-year-old), two juvenile (16–17-year-old), and 21 junior (18–19-year-old)
- 1992 Senior National champion 52 kg
- Member of the Senior National Team from 1989 to 1996
- Three-time silver medalist at the Pan American Championships
- Bronze medalist at the 1993 World Cup
- Silver medalist at the 1994 Francophone Games
- 1987 World Youth Wrestling champion—junior freestyle 46 kg

- 1996 Olympic team member—eighth at the Atlanta Olympics 52 kg
- Coached high school wrestling from 1994 to 2005 for the GEDSB and the HWDSB
- On the OFSAA wrestling tournament organizing committee in 1993, 1994, and 1995
- Executive member of SOSSA for all sports from 2002 to present
- Currently the administrative rep for the SOSSA committee (principal's rep)
- Inducted into the McMaster University Athletic Hall of Fame, 2006

Kimberly Ann Elizabeth Ribble, Judo Fighter

In the early 1990s, it appeared that only grappling mattered in the full-contact MMA arena. Then, in the late 1990s it started to seem like kickboxing and grappling were the two major phases of combat. Now we know that the clinch is probably the trickiest part of the fight because it determines whether the fight stays standing or goes to the ground, and it decides who is going to start in top position on the ground when it goes there. To understand the clinch, who better to ask than experienced judo fighters and wrestlers? Kimberly Ribble, a world-class judoka, has also been very helpful by providing a woman's perspective on fighting.

ACCOMPLISHMENTS

- Began judo when she was seven, soccer when she was nine, water polo when she was fourteen
- Represented Canada for twelve years as a National Team member
- Competed and medaled around the world in the following weight categories: 66 kg, 72 kg, and 78 kg (her Olympic weight)
- Multiple-time Canadian champion

- Four-time U.S Open medalist
- British Open silver medal
- Commonwealth gold, silver, and bronze medalist
- Pan American silver and bronze medalist
- Hungarian Cup bronze medal
- Represented Canada at the 2000 Sydney Olympic Games
- NCCP level 3 coach
- Coached both senior and junior provincial teams and has twice coached for the Canada Winter Games

David Malar, Judo Coach

David Malar, born into an intensely athletic and competitive family, had a successful competitive swimming career prior to discovering the combat sports, and judo in particular. Known as a very tough fighter, his interest in the combat arts has focused on self-defense and mixed martial arts training. He is a highly respected coach at the Hamilton School of Martial Arts.

ACCOMPLISHMENTS

- Began training in judo in 1989 at the age of eighteen
- Was promoted to black belt by Judo Canada in 1999
- Focus has always been on the full martial arts range of judo rather than strictly competition judo rules
- Has additionally trained in full-contact freestyle fighting and weaponry
- Coaching since 1996 and founder and head instructor of Kakure Judo Club at the Hamilton School of Martial Arts
- Holds NCCP level 2 judo coaching certification

Robert Kranstz, Sports Promoter, Coach, and Competitor

There are few people today who can claim to have created an international sport. Robert Kranstz is one of those few. In 1977, in Hawaii, he collaborated with Ron Forrester to establish the International Sport Jiu-Jitsu Championships, one of the very first mixed martial arts tournaments in the modern Western world, long before MMA became anything remotely close to a household topic of discussion. The Sport Jiu-Jitsu World Championships is today one of a small number of major international amateur MMA events, held every three years, with many countries holding their own national championships annually using the same rules. Along with devising, testing, and putting into practice the rules for this internationally successful form of mixed martial arts, Kranstz created a pedagogical system for teaching all the phases of combat together, which he named the Combined Jiu-Jitsu Arts (CJA) system. This too was ahead of its time, in that it took the approach that hand-to-hand combat is made up of several distinct phases and skill sets that need to be trained separately and then combined, rather than only one. As well as being the founder and CEO of the CJA, Robart Kranstz holds a black belt in judo and a seventh dan in Jiu-Jitsu, is a three-time amateur mixed martial arts world champion, and has coached four national teams to first place at the Worlds. He retired as a correctional officer in 2005 and now devotes all his time to promoting and coaching amateur MMA and teaching the Combined Jiu-Jitsu Arts.

Index

Page numbers followed by *f* indicate a figure.

About the Authors

Mickey Dimic, Mixed Martial Artist, Coach, and Author

Mickey Dimic has thirty-four years of experience in martial arts. A two-time world middleweight champion, he is currently the head coach for the Canadian Jiu-Jitsu Association. He has trained seven world champions and has a school with approximately four hundred students. He also teaches street defense and self-defense classes for younger students. He is an active MMA competitor.

FIGHTING CAREER

- Fifth dan Jiu-Jitsu
- Started Jiu-Jitsu in 1979
- Began competing immediately in Jiu-Jitsu amateur MMA tourneys and also in wrestling and kickboxing
- Started his own club in 1991 called the Hamilton School of Martial Arts
- In the Canadian Jiu-Jitsu Championships, took second in 1992 and first in 1993, 1994, 1995, 1996, and 1997
- Won the team event at the U.S. Championships in 1994
- In 1995 in New Zealand at the Worlds, took second in the team event and fifth in the individuals category
- Won the International Sport Jiu-Jitsu Championships 1996 World Championships in the middleweight category, held in Virginia
- Won the Fighter of the Year award in 1997

- Took a second at the Jiu-Jitsu World Championships at Reno, Nevada, in 1998
- Took a second at the Jiu-Jitsu World Championships at Quebec in 1999
- Won the ISJJ World Championships for a second time in 2004
- Also in 2004 was inducted into the World Martial Arts Hall of Fame

TEACHING, COACHING, AND COMMUNITY HIGHLIGHTS

- Hosted fourteen Canadian Championship Tournaments
- Teaches a Mohawk College credit course for law and security
- Teaches self-defense at secondary schools
- Teaches street-proofing for kids at elementary schools
- Gives self-defense seminars
- Volunteers for the YMCA and City of Hamilton teaching self-defense for abused women
- Holds a yearly Kick-a-thon to raise money for Sick Kids Hospital, the Children's Hospital, and Cancer Child
- In 1998 coached two amateur students from his club to win World Champion titles: Mark Simon (lightweight) and Mike Childs (heavyweight); Mark won again in 2004
- In 2001, coached the Canadian grappling team at the Worlds in France
- In 2007, coached the Canadian team that earned a silver medal at the Worlds in the Channel Islands
- At the Jiu-Jitsu Worlds in 2007, his student Adam Hensen became amateur world champion in MMA

JUDO

- Started judo in 1974
- Started competing right away three months later; won his first tournament
- Loved competing; used to have a monthly club shiai tourney at the Hamilton Kodokan: made sure he never missed one

- Won the Fighter of the Year award at the club every year
- Stayed with judo for seventeen years, competing
- Won fourteen regionals
- Won three Ontario judo championships
- Won three Can-Ams
- In the Canadian championships, placed fifth in 1983, third in 1984, and second in 1985

Christopher Miller, Fighter and Writer

A judo black belt, Chris Miller started training in the sport at the age of eleven. As much a scholar as a fighter, he has always been fascinated with the science of full-contact fighting. This passion led him to studying in-depth a number of combat sports—judo, submission grappling, fencing, kendo, kickboxing, and mixed martial arts—in North America and Asia. A successful national and international-level competitor with podium finishes in major judo, submission grappling, and amateur MMA events, he trains under David Malar and Mickey Dimic at the Hamilton School of Martial Arts. He is equally passionate about historical literature and was granted a master's degree in classical literature by the University of Western Ontario in 2004. His paper entitled *Submission Fighting and the Rules of Ancient Greek Wrestling* established for the first time in the modern era what the rules for ancient Greek and Roman wrestling were, based on a thorough analysis of original source documents. He is a devoted secondary school teacher, instructing history, the social sciences, and analytical writing to avid, dedicated students of the disciplines in Dundas, Ontario, Canada.